MEN-AT-ARMS SERIES

EDITOR: MARTIN WINDROW

Battle for the Falklands (1) Land Forces

Text by

WILLIAM FOWLER

Colour plates by

MICHAEL CHAPPELL

OSPREY PUBLISHING LONDON

Published in 1982 by
Osprey Publishing Ltd
Member company of the George Philip Group
12–14 Long Acre, London WC2E 9LP
© Copyright 1982 Osprey Publishing Ltd
Reprinted 1983
Reprinted and revised 1983 (twice),
1984, 1985, 1987 (twice)

British Library Cataloguing in Publication Data

Battle for the Falklands.—(Men-at-arms series; 133)
  1: Land forces
  1. Falkland Islands War, 1982
  I. Fowler, William   II. Series
  997.11   F30311

ISBN 0-85045-482-4

Filmset in England by
Tameside Filmsetting Limited,
Ashton-under-Lyne, Lancashire

Printed in Hong Kong

Author's note:
The author wishes to record his gratitude to the following
for their generous help in the preparation of this book;
Public Relations Dept., Ministry of Defence; Globe and
Laurel; Gunner; The Royal United Services Institute;
The Sunday Times; The Daily Telegraph; Time
Magazine; Peter Abbott; John Chappell; Geoff Cornish;
Simon Dunstan; Adrian English; Paul Haley; Lee
Russell; and Digby Smith. Under the circumstances the
publishers feel it may be desirable to note that a donation
has been made to the South Atlantic Fund.

This book is dedicated to Christine, for her patience
and good company during the events described within.

Introduction

'I remember just before the battle of Antietam thinking . . . that it would be easy after a comfortable breakfast to come down the steps of one's house pulling on one's gloves and smoking a cigar, to get on to a horse and charge a battery up Beacon Street, while the ladies wave handkerchiefs from a balcony. But the reality was to pass a night on the ground in the rain, with your bowels out of order, and then, after no particular breakfast, to wade a stream and attack the enemy'.
(Oliver Wendell Holmes Jr, recalling his service in the American Civil War)

With the lethal tidying-up of the Falklands battlefield still in progress and claiming lives and limbs, millions of words have already been written and spoken about Operation 'Corporate', the combined service operations that liberated the islanders from Argentine occupation. Inevitably, much remains to be revealed; this book can only be a summary of what is known at the time of writing. Perhaps more important is its other purpose. The view of war from a Press desk, radio station or television studio is often a cosily sanitised version of what is in reality a grinding mixture of fatigue, confusion and ignorance at all levels; of moments of great fear, and others of intense exhilaration; and of a tough humour that welds close-knit groups closer still under pressure. I hope that this brief account will convey something of this reality, so eloquently recalled by Oliver Wendell Holmes when he looked back on his own war.

* * *

There is no space here for more than the briefest note on the background to the war. The Falkland Islands and their dependency of South Georgia are a group of rocky, barren islands in the south-west corner of the South Atlantic Ocean. They have a population of about 1,800 souls, 1,000 of them living in the little 'capital' of Stanley and the remainder scattered around the heavily indented coasts in isolated, more or less self-sufficient sheep farming settlements.

The islands have never been settled by the Argentine, although for a brief period during the confused years which saw her war of independence from Spain she did plant a minute garrison on them. This was removed, bloodlessly, by Britain in 1833; since when settlement by civilians has slowly increased, the inhabitants being entirely of British stock. Argentina's notional claim is based upon proximity, and a supposed sovereignty which ultimately rests upon the Papal declaration of 1493 which sought arbitrarily to divide the unoccupied discoveries in the New World between Spain and Portugal—a pronouncement which failed to impress the rest of the world even then. Resting her

(Cont. on p. 5)

2 April: a LARC-5 vehicle of the Argentine Marines' 1st Amphibious Vehicle Bn. approaches as Royal Marines of NP8901 are searched by Argentine Marine Commandos. This is one of a series of photographs which had a considerable effect on British public opinion. (MoD)

Chronology

19 March 1982   Argentine scrap merchants land on South Georgia and raise flag. Diplomatic exchanges begin.

2 April   Argentine Marine forces invade East Falkland. After three-hour fight, 67-man Royal Marine garrison ordered to surrender by Governor Hunt.

3 April   United Nations Security Council passes Resolution 502, calling on Argentina to withdraw troops. Argentine Marines force surrender of 22-man garrison of South Georgia, after two Argentine helicopters shot down and a frigate badly damaged.

5 April   First warships of British Task Force sail from UK. Lord Carrington and two junior Foreign Office ministers resign.

7 April   Announcement of 200-mile Exclusion Zone around Falklands, to become effective 12 April, by Ministry of Defence in London.

25 April   Argentine submarine *Santa Fé* damaged by RN helicopters and forced to beach at Grytviken, South Georgia. 25/26 April, South Georgia recaptured by 22 SAS Regt. and 42 Cdo.RM.

30 April   US diplomatic mediation abandoned; US government announces unequivocal support of Britain.

1 May   RAF Vulcan and Task Force Harriers attack Stanley airport in first of many raids.

2 May   ARA *General Belgrano* sunk by RN submarine.

4 May   HMS *Sheffield* struck by Argentine air-launched Exocet missile and burns out, sinking later.

7 May   Announcement of extension of Total Exclusion Zone to within 12 miles of Argentine coast.

14 May   22 SAS Regt. raid Argentine airfield on Pebble Island.

21 May   Task Force establishes beachhead at San Carlos on East Falkland. HMS *Ardent* sunk by Argentine air attack. At least 14 Argentine aircraft shot down.

23 May   HMS *Antelope* crippled by air attack, sinks next day. At least six aircraft shot down.

24 May   Air attacks continue; eight aircraft shot down.

25 May   Air attacks continue. HMS *Coventry* sunk; *Atlantic Conveyor*, carrying important stores and helicopters, struck by air-launched Exocet and burns out. Several Argentine aircraft shot down.

26 May   British troops move out of beachhead on two routes.

28 May   2nd Bn. The Parachute Regt. takes Goose Green and Darwin in prolonged fighting. Survivors of 1,400-strong Argentine garrison surrender to 600 paratroopers the next morning.

31 May   Troops of 42 Cdo.RM established on Mt. Kent.

2 June   British troops in sight of Stanley.

8 June   Argentine air attack on LSLs *Sir Tristram* and *Sir Galahad* at Fitzroy; heavy casualties among 1st Bn. The Welsh Guards.

11/12 June   Series of night attacks on high ground west of Stanley; Mt. Longdon, Two Sisters and Mt. Harriet captured. Land-launched Exocet missile strikes HMS *Glamorgan* but damage controlled.

13/14 June   Tumbledown, Mt. William and Wireless Ridge taken in night attacks. Argentine troops flee final positions before Stanley. White flags seen. Argentine commander, Gen. Menéndez, agrees to parley with Maj.Gen. Moore.

14 June   Unconditional surrender of Argentine troops on Falklands at 2059hrs local time.

claim upon unbroken occupation, administration, and national settlement since 1833, Britain has offered to submit the dispute to the International Court of Justice—an offer declined by Argentina. Her claim is taught as holy writ in Argentine schools, however, and generations of Argentines have been raised to believe it implicitly. It has an emotional significance for them at least equal to the responsibility Britain feels toward the liberties of the islanders, or 'kelpers' as they are nicknamed, from the thick beds of seaweed which blanket the shores. The fact that the islanders have always made clear their determination to retain their British identity and liberties has not silenced Argentine rhetoric about 'colonialism'.

The British Foreign and Commonwealth Office has long recognised the practical benefits, both to the islanders and to Britain, of a good working relationship between the Falklanders and the Argentine; but the islanders' understandable reluctance to fall into the hands of an immature and unstable country currently ruled by a military dictatorship with a horrific record of secret police kidnappings, tortures and murders has prevented the long-drawn negotiations from bearing fruit. In early 1982 the announcement of the imminent withdrawal of the Royal Navy's ice patrol ship HMS *Endurance*, and various other marks of apparent inattention, prompted the current military Junta in Buenos Aires to suppose that a military grab would be allowed to succeed without more than token resistance. Such an adventure was attractive as a distraction for the Argentine public at a time of soaring inflation and political unease.

A *causus belli* was engineered by the planting of a party of supposed 'scrap merchants' on South Georgia, whose ostensibly innocent presence was compromised by the raising of the Argentine flag, and the tiny Royal Marine force despatched 22 men to South Georgia's port of Grytviken to keep an eye on the Argentine party at Leith. It was at this point in what seemed a trivial dispute that, on the night of 1/2 April 1982, the Junta led by Gen. Leopoldo Galtieri made its move. On 3 April British Prime Minister Mrs. Margaret Thatcher faced an appalled and furious House of Commons to announce that Argentine armed forces had landed on British sovereign territory; had captured the men of Royal Marine detachment NP8901; had run up

3 Para practising helicopter drill with Sea Kings on the SS *Canberra* **during the Task Force's voyage south; they wear life jackets and '58 pattern CEFO. Helmet camouflage is to personal taste. (MoD)**

the Argentine flag at Government House; and had declared the islands and their population to be Argentine.

The Invasion

In fact, local indications gave the tiny RM garrison a couple of days' warning. The arrival of Maj. Mike Norman's detachment to relieve the 1980–81 detachment of Maj. Gary Noott gave the islands' governor, Mr. Rex Hunt, a total force of 67 men armed with infantry weapons, including the General Purpose Machine Gun, the 66mm anti-tank rocket launcher, and the 84mm Carl Gustav anti-tank weapon. Maj. Norman assumed command on 1 April, and deployed his men at key points.

The airfield is on a headland east of the town of Stanley, joined to it by a narrow isthmus along which runs a surfaced road. While the airfield had been obstructed, two beaches north of it were considered likely landing points; and it was along the enemy's only axis of advance from this direction that four of the sections were deployed, with orders to delay that advance and to withdraw when the pressure became too great. No.5 Section (Cpl. Duff) was south of the airfield, with a GPMG team covering the beach. At Hookers Point on the isthmus was No.1 Section (Cpl. Armour); behind them were No.2 (Cpl. Brown) on the old airstrip, and No.3 (Cpl. Johnson) near the immobilised VOR directional beacon.

No. 4 Section (Cpl. York) were placed at the narrow harbour entrance with a Gemini assault boat, and ordered to resist any naval attempt to enter the harbour. The MV *Forrest* was put on radar watch in Port William, the outer harbour. No.6 Section covered the south of the town from Murray Heights, with an OP on Sapper Hill. Main HQ were at Government House, on the west of the town, where Maj. Noott assisted Mr. Hunt; Maj. Norman, in overall command, was at Look Out Rocks. Mr. Hunt had ordered that there should be no fighting in the town itself, to safeguard civilian lives.

In the early hours of 2 April *Forrest* reported contacts off Mengary Point and Cape Pembroke, and helicopters were heard near Port Harriet. Argentine accounts would later identify these contacts as the aircraft carrier *Veinticinco de Mayo*,

2 Para personnel test-fire GPMG and SLRs over the stern of the *Norland* ferry during the voyage south. At this stage a rather light-hearted attitude prevailed, as few believed the Task Force would be sent into battle in earnest. (MoD)

the destroyers *Hercules*, *Segui* and *Comodoro Py*, the landing ship *Cabo San Antonio*, and three transports. The force they carried was reported as 600 Marines and 279 Army and Air Force personnel, a battalion of amphibious APCs, and Marine Commando special forces including frogmen.

Argentine sources place the first landing at Cape Pembroke, where frogmen landing from assault craft secured the lighthouse and its small RM observation post. The first landing recorded by the British was by a heli-borne force of 150 Marines near Mullet Creek, tasked with neutralising any defenders of the Moody Brook RM barracks and then moving on to capture the governor. They were shortly afterwards reinforced by another 70 men, all being landed by Sea Kings from the carrier. At between 0530 and 0605—sources differ—they reached the empty barracks, and proceeded to clear it with automatic fire and white phosphorous grenades: odd tactics for troops who would later be claimed to have 'used blank ammunition to save lives'. The noise of this attack alerted the men around Government House. Both sides agree that the firefight there began at 0615.

It was to last for three hours, while the dawn broke and brightened. Argentine figures for casualties were one killed and two wounded. Royal Marine estimates were rather higher, but could not be confirmed: five dead and 17 wounded.

Even in the grimmest moments there can be humour, as when the section covering the harbour called in that it had three targets to engage with its GPMG, and asked, 'What are the priorities?'

'What are the targets?', came the reply from HQ.

'Target No.1 is an aircraft carrier, Target No.2 is a cruiser, Target . . .', at which point the line went dead. The harbour section in fact managed to evade capture for four days after the invasion.

Lt. C. W. Trollope, with Sgt. Sheppard, was at the old airfield with No. 2 Section, and at 0630 reported ships to the south. Moments later he heard tracked vehicles, and was soon able to count 16 LVTP-7s of the Argentine Marines 1st Amphibious Vehicles Bn. coming over the ridge from York Bay. As the section withdrew in the face of these formidable vehicles, which have a turret-mounted 12.7mm machine gun, Marine Gibbs stopped the lead APC with a 66mm hit on the passenger compartment, while Marines Brown and Best put a

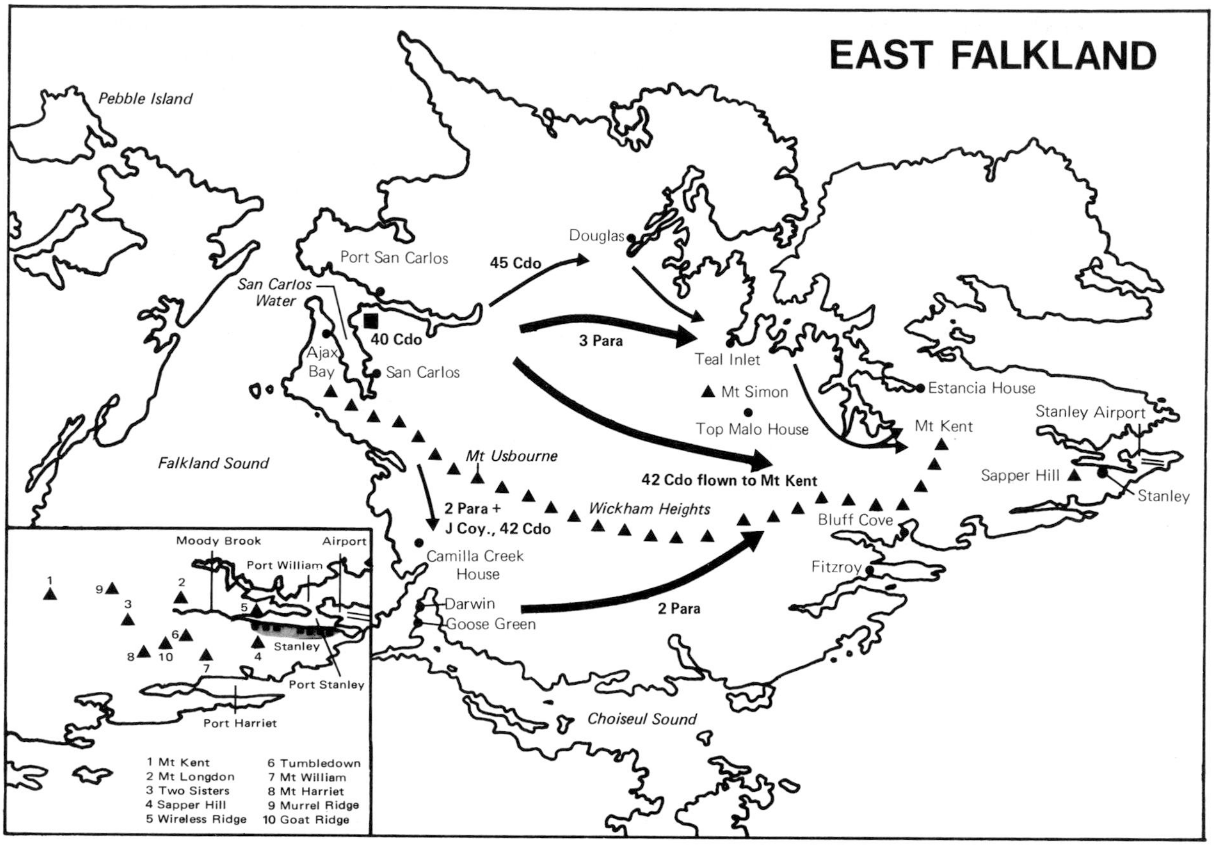
EAST FALKLAND
Pebble Island
Port San Carlos
45 Cdo
Douglas
San Carlos Water
40 Cdo
3 Para
Ajax Bay
San Carlos
Teal Inlet
Mt Simon
Estancia House
Top Malo House
Mt Kent
Stanley Airport
Falkland Sound
Mt Usbourne
42 Cdo flown to Mt Kent
Sapper Hill
Stanley
2 Para +
J Coy., 42 Cdo
Wickham Heights
Bluff Cove
Camilla Creek House
Fitzroy
Darwin
Goose Green
2 Para
Choiseul Sound
Moody Brook
Airport
Port William
Stanley
Port Stanley
Port Harriet
1 Mt Kent
2 Mt Longdon
3 Two Sisters
4 Sapper Hill
5 Wireless Ridge
6 Tumbledown
7 Mt William
8 Mt Harriet
9 Murrel Ridge
10 Goat Ridge

round of 84mm through the front. 'No one was seen to surface . . .' The other APCs deployed to open fire, and the section fell back again.

By 0830, with Argentine troops clearly ashore in great numbers, Maj. Norman and Mr. Hunt looked at the options. These included an attempt at escape and evasion into the interior, where the governor could set up an alternative seat of government; or a firefight that would be 'determined, unrelenting, but relatively short-lived'. The governor, who was commander-in-chief under the Emergency Powers Ordnance of 1939, decided on the depressing option of surrender to save civilian lives.

For the Argentine forces it was a moment of triumph. The sky blue and white national flag was run up on every pole in sight. An Iwo Jima-style scenario of Marines grouped around a flag pole at dawn was followed by a more formal parade for the cameras, with Marine Commandos in their knitted caps and quilted jackets forming one side of a hollow square, and others in camouflage uniforms facing them.

Mr. Hunt declined to join these ceremonies, or even to shake hands with Gen. Oswaldo Garcia, 'temporary military governor of the Malvinas', and Adm. Carlos Busser, commander of the Marine Corps. Mustering his full diplomatic dignity, he was driven off to the airfield for evacuation to the United Kingdom via Montevideo, complete with plumed hat and sword. The Royal Marines were to follow the same route rather later.

It was to prove a Pyrrhic victory for Argentina. The photos of the young Royal Marines, tired faces smeared with camouflage cream, being disarmed and marched off by an equally young but rather officious Argentine Commando caused great public anger in Britain. Rightly or wrongly, the British public finds the image of British troops with their hands up inflaming. It was this rather forlorn image which made the Task Force politically acceptable—even inevitable.

South Georgia

Under normal circumstances a lieutenant is never likely to have a wholly independent command—let alone the scrutiny of the world while he exercises it.

Lt. Keith Mills, OC the 22-man RM detachment aboard the ice patrol vessel HMS *Endurance*, was summoned by Capt. N. J. Barker on 31 March and ordered to (a) be a military presence on the island of South Georgia; (b) protect the British Antarctic Survey party at Grytviken in the event of an emergency; and (c) to maintain surveillance over the Argentine 'scrap merchants' at Leith, a derelict whaling station.

Radio transmissions from Stanley left them in no doubt that they would be next. The Argentine vessel *Bahia Paraiso*, with its own Marine detachment, was known to be in the area. Lt. Mills selected a position at King Edward Point covering approaches to Grytviken; he also picked a withdrawal route, along which the Marines stashed their 'E and E' kits and rucksacks. They wired the beach, and booby-trapped the jetty and the approaches to their position.

At 1230 on 2 April the *Bahia Paraiso* made a fleeting appearance. Next day she returned, sending a message announcing the surrender of the 'Malvinas' and the dependencies. Mills played for

As tracers rise into the dusk sky, soldiers man an improvised .50cal. MG position on a cargo container lashed to the deck of the *Canberra*. (Paul Haley, 'Soldier' Magazine)

time, reading this back using an HF net which allowed the Royal Navy and BAS call signs to hear as well. The Argentines called on the defenders to assemble on the beach to surrender. By now the frigate *Granville* had entered the bay, and a helicopter was overhead. The *Bahia Paraiso* was informed that there was a British military presence on the island, with orders to resist a landing. A further attempt at stalling failed, and a second helicopter appeared. The frigate headed for the open sea again; one of the helicopters landed, and eight Argentine Marines jumped out 40 yards from Lt. Mills. One of them took aim, and Mills returned to his defensive position. The Argentines opened fire, and another helicopter dropped troops on the far side of the bay, who opened up with machine guns. The Royal Marines now returned fire.

Their automatic bursts ripped into the Puma helicopter, which lurched across the bay trailing smoke, and crash-landed on the far side; nobody emerged. Two Alouette helicopters which landed troops across the bay were engaged, and one of them was hit, landing heavily and taking no further part in the action. This was already a respectable engagement; but the Royal Marines were now to

achieve a success unique in the campaign. The frigate headed back to shore and began to give fire support to the Argentine troops; she had a 3.9in. gun, but seems to have used her twin 40mm on this occasion. Lt. Mills ordered his men to hold fire until she was well within the bay, with less chance of taking swift evasive action; and then hit her with the 84mm anti-tank weapon.

Fired by Marine Dave Combes, the Carl Gustav round hit the water about ten yards short of the ship and ricochetted into the hull, holing it close to the waterline. The frigate turned to avoid further fire, and while it did so it was raked with MG and rifle fire, more than 1,000 hits being reported later by an Argentine officer. At least two 66mm LAW rounds hit near the forward turret, jamming its elevation mechanism; and, according to one report, a second 84mm round may have struck the Exocet launchers abaft the funnel, which fortunately for the crew did not explode. Rapidly retreating beyond small arms range, the *Granville* continued to fire in support of the troops who were closing in to outflank the British position.

After causing a number of casualties, and with retreat cut off except down the steep cliffs, Lt. Mills took the initiative to parley with an enemy officer. He pointed out that since each side had the other pinned down, both would inevitably suffer heavily if the action continued; to avoid this he was prepared to surrender. He had a wounded man, and he had achieved his aim of forcing the invaders to use force. He had also guaranteed good treatment for his men. They had a long sea journey to an Argentine base, and a further four days' confinement, before being flown to Montevideo and on to Britain, with the section from Stanley harbour who had avoided capture on 2 April. Lt. Mills was later awarded the DSC.

The Task Force and its Opponents

In Britain there was considerable national anger at the invasion. Apart from the humiliation of seeing Royal Marines marched off as prisoners, there were the transmitted voices of the islanders: part West

Men of 42 Commando, Royal Marines at Grytviken. M Company—'The Mighty Munch'—recaptured South Georgia alongside men of D Sqn., 22 SAS Regt. on 25 April. (MoD)

Country, part Midland, but wholly British. The thought of their misfortune had a powerful impact. Some voices of dissent were heard from the extreme Left as the Task Force was prepared, but these were confined to an entirely predictable quarter, and the degree of publicity they attracted—particularly in Buenos Aires—was quite unrepresentative of national feeling. It is hard to imagine any other issue which could attract more than 80 per cent unanimous support for government action in opinion polls.

The recall of the men of the Royal Marines and 3 Para came as something of a surprise. Dramatic announcements and chalked signs aroused the

Lt.Cdr. Alfredo Astiz of the Argentine Navy, wearing Marines camouflage clothing and the blue-grey winter SD cap of a naval officer, signs the surrender of the enemy garrison on South Georgia on board HMS *Plymouth*, watched by Capt. N. J. Barker of HMS *Endurance* (right) and Capt. D. Pentreath of *Plymouth* (far right). (MoD)

LCMs from HMS *Fearless* head towards Blue Beach, San Carlos with men of 40 Cdo.RM on the morning of 21 May. (MoD)

curiosity of commuters at London stations. In 45 Commando there was some difficulty in convincing men due for Easter leave that this was not some horrible April Fool's joke. As one group were informed: 'Now listen, men, the good news—there isn't any. The bad news—Argentina has invaded the Falkland Islands. Everyone has been recalled. Your leave has hereby been *cancelled*.'

The Task Force carrier group set sail on Monday 5 April, and by the evening of Friday the 9th SS *Canberra* was putting to sea with the main body of 40 and 42 Commandos and 3 Para; 45 Cdo. were accommodated aboard the RFA *Stromness*, RFA *Resource* and two LSLs which sailed at intervals over a week. As *Canberra* eased away from the dock at Southampton she was cheered by a vast crowd of relatives and well-wishers, and military bands serenaded her departure with the Gavin Sutherland song 'Sailing'. (This has become so popular since the Rod Stewart recording was used as the signature tune for a successful TV documentary series about HMS *Ark Royal* that it is almost an unofficial anthem for Britain's maritime forces.)

Another song which now has associations with the departure of troops for the Falklands is Tim Rice and Andrew Lloyd Webber's 'Don't Cry For Me, Argentina'—quickly modified by some wits to the more bellicose 'Don't *Try* For Me, Argentina'; it was to these ironic strains that 2 Para left their Aldershot barracks. The battalion was accommodated aboard the *Europic Ferry* and the MV *Norland*. Like the men of the Royal Artillery, Royal Engineers and Blues and Royals, aboard other Royal Fleet Auxiliary and Merchant Marine vessels, they began a period of intensive onboard training. The Blues and Royals were aboard *Elk*—a transport whose master, like many of his breed, was soon to display an impressively warlike spirit, demanding ever more machine guns to jury-rig all over his ship!—and had with them four Scimitar and two Scorpion light tanks forming Medium Recce Troop, B Squadron, and one Samson ARV.

The real surprise came when the government announced that the liner *Queen Elizabeth 2* was to be requisitioned on 1 May. She would carry the men of 5 Infantry Brigade—2nd Bn. The Scots Guards, 1st Bn. The Welsh Guards, 1st Bn. 7th Gurkha Rifles, and their supporting units—who would reinforce 3 Cdo.Bde., which now consisted of the three RM Cdos. with 2 and 3 Para attached. Their vehicles would be carried by the *Baltic Ferry* and *Nordic Ferry*, their artillery and stores by *Atlantic Causeway*. Before embarking 5 Inf.Bde. went to the Sennybridge training area in Wales to bring themselves to peak efficiency, using live ammunition and live air attacks. It was hoped that the notoriously rainy weather in the area would simulate the Falklands climate as closely as possible. On cue, central Wales obliged with a minor heatwave.

The *QE2*, converted to take helicopters, sailed on 12 May. She nosed out of Southampton on a sunny Wednesday; families and friends, many of the women in tears, waved to the soldiers lining the decks. The intensely moving occasion was slightly deflated when one serviceman's wife brought a delighted roar from the troops by stripping to the waist, and her bra was swung aboard the stately liner to yells of approval.

* * *

The preparation and despatch of the Task Force came as a surprise to the Argentine Junta. In that male-dominated society Mrs. Thatcher's response was seen as a typically female overreaction. While US Secretary of State Haig pursued his exhausting shuttle diplomacy, the Argentine enjoyed a surge of national pride. Although there were many, both in Buenos Aires and Britain, who could not believe that the Task Force would be used in earnest, the Junta took the precaution of reinforcing the islands. After their defeat they were to claim that they had been beaten by a high-technology nation: examination of their weapons and equipment showed almost the opposite.

With military men heading the government, the forces were subject to fewer financial constraints than their opposite numbers. They had shopped well in Europe and the USA, and though some of their warships were old the armour, artillery and infantry weapons were good. The garrison had 30 105mm and four 155mm guns, of Italian and French origins respectively. Their mortars included 81mm and heavy 120mm types. They had excellent Swiss 35mm and German 20mm twin AA cannon mountings, some at least with Skyguard radar; AA missile launchers included the French Roland and British Tigercat, and the British Blowpipe man-portable system. It came as a nasty surprise to the men of the Task Force to discover that not only was much of the electronic equipment superior to their own—but some of the better pieces were British-built. One piece of Direction Finding equipment could locate a transmitter after it had been on the air for a matter of seconds.

Particularly ironic was one Argentine claim, in the aftermath of defeat, that British night-fighting aids were of unprecedented sophistication. The aids used by Argentine troops were a generation ahead of British equipment. Testing a captured set of the 'goggles', which could be worn with ease by a foot soldier, an officer of 2 Para was able to identify by name a man looking through a house window— whose glass degrades vision—across 30 metres of street and through a second window, at night. The night sights for the Argentine FN rifles were lighter and more compact than British equivalents, and the scale of issue meant that more were available to an Argentine platoon.

To cover against air and sea attack the garrison had Westinghouse AN/TPS-43 mobile radar sets valued at around £6 million, and land-based versions of the French Exocet anti-ship missile. Light armour was provided by 12 French Panhard AML armoured cars with 90mm guns; these wheeled vehicles were reckoned to be more suitable after the Marines' APCs had cut up Stanley's roads, but in fact they played little or no part in the fighting. Most, perhaps all of the LVTP-7s seem to have left the islands before the liberation, but when Stanley fell the Task Force captured about 150 trucks and jeeps.

A photograph that for many people summed up the essential point of the campaign; above the San Carlos landing beaches, RSM Laurie Ashbridge of 3 Para enjoys a cup of tea with delighted local families. (MoD)

With their numerous grass strips for private aircraft and the 'flying doctor', the Falklands were ideal for helicopters and STOL aircraft. The enemy air forces flew in at least twelve Pumas, two Chinooks, nine Bell 'Hueys' and two Agusta A109 gunships. Up to two dozen turbo-prop Pucará COIN aircraft were dispersed at Stanley, Goose Green and Pebble Island; with its good STOL performance and mix of cannon and under-wing ordnance, it was a formidable battlefield support machine.

At the individual level the troops were armed with the FN rifle, some with a folding stock, and all with a burst or automatic capability. The machine guns were the FN/MAG, almost identical to the British GPMG, and, at squad level, the heavy-barrel FN. Hand grenades were from a number of origins, but soldiers who have been on the receiving end said that they functioned effectively. Although one elegant dress sword was captured at San Carlos, the officers' normal sidearm was the 9mm Browning pistol.

The British Task Force was described as 'a well balanced force', but the same could also be said of the Argentine garrison pouring into the Falklands. As the heavy equipment was put ashore at the harbour the troops were flown into Stanley, and plodded off to their temporary accommodation—mostly pup-tents—laden with packs, kit bags and weapons. They were a mixture of conscripts, some of whom were reported to be only beginning their service, and more experienced soldiers. The Press stories about 15 year-olds in the ranks should be weighed against the fact that the most recent call-up

British Land Forces in Operation 'Corporate'

3 Commando Brigade Royal Marines
40 Commando RM
42 Commando RM
45 Commando RM
29 (Commando) Regt., Royal Artillery
148 Cdo.FO Bty., RA
59 Independent Cdo.Sqn., Royal Engineers
Cdo. Logistic Regt., RM
3 Cdo.Bde.HQ & Signals Sqn., RM
3 Cdo.Bde. Air Sqn., RM—Gazelle & Scout helicopters
1 Raiding Sqn., RM—Rigid Raiding Craft and Gemini
2, 4 & 6 Sections, Special Boat Squadron, RM
Mountain & Arctic Warfare Cadre, RM
Nos. 845 & 846 Naval Air Sqns.—Sea King helicopters
Landing Ships Logistic & Mexefloat Detachments
Y Troop, RM Signals
SATCOM Dets., Royal Signals
49 Explosive Ordnance Device Sqn., RE
Surgical Support Team, Royal Navy
Cdo. Forces Band, RM—medical duties

Army Units attached to 3 Cdo.Bde. for 'Corporate'
3rd Bn. The Parachute Regt.
Medium Recce Tp., B Sqn., The Blues and Royals—4 Scorpion, 4 Scimitar, 1 Samson
T Bty., 12 Air Defence Regt., RA—12 Rapier SAM
FOO Parties, 4 Field Regt., RA
RLD, 30 Sigs.Regt., RSigs
Sect., 19 Fd.Amb., RAMC/RADC

5 Infantry Brigade
2nd Bn. The Scots Guards
1st Bn. The Welsh Guards
2nd Bn. The Parachute Regiment
1st Bn., 7th Gurkha Rifles
4 Fd.Regt., RA (—)
2 Tps., 32 Guided Weapons Regt., RA
FOO Parties, 49 Fd.Regt./Royal School of Artillery Support Regt., RA
36 Engr.Regt., RE(—)
9 Para Sqn., RE
Det., 2 Port Control Regt., RE

No. 656 Sqn., Army Air Corps—Gazelle & Scout helicopters
407 Transport Tp., Royal Corps of Transport
Elements, 17 Port Regt., RCT
16 Fd.Amb., RAMC
81 Ordnance Coy., RAOC
Laundry/Bakery Det., 9 Ord.Bn., RAOC
Elms., 421 EOD Coy., RAOC/RE
10 Forward Workshop, REME
160 Provo Coy., RMP
6 Fd.Cash Office, RAPC
PR Det

Force Troops
Army Elms., HQ LFFI
12 AD Regt., RA
21 AD Bty., 27 Fd.Regt., RA
11 Sqn., 38 Engr.Regt., RE
EOD Det., 33 Engr.Regt., RE
Det., 38 Engr.Regt., RE
Det., 2 PC Regt., RE
Elms., Mil. Works Force, RPC
Det., 11 Ord.Bn., RAOC
Det., 14 Sigs.Regt., RSigs
Dets., 30 Sigs.Regt., RSigs
D Sqn. and G Sqn., 22 SAS Regt.
Elms., No.657 Sqn., AAC—Gazelle & Scout helicopters
172 Int. & Secty.Sect., Int.Corps(—)
Elms., 17 Port Regt., RCT
Elms., Joint Heli.Serv.Unit, RAF
Elms., 29 Mov.Regt., RCT/REME

Ascension Island
Elms., 22 Engr.Regt., RE
Elms., 38 Engr.Regt., RE
Elms., Mil.Works Force, RPC
Det., 2 PC Regt., RE
Det., 30 Sigs.Regt., RSigs
47 Air Despatch Sqn., RCT
Laundry Det., 9 Ord.Bn., RAOC
Det., 4 Petrol Depot, RAOC
Det., 49 Rp Coy.
Misc. RAOC, ACC

category were 19 year-olds of the 1962/63 register. (Most Task Force soldiers were aged between 18 and 25 years.)

The engineers began a vast obstacle construction operation to deny the British routes out from their likely landing areas. The Argentine assessment was that the British would go for Stanley in a *coup de main* which would ensure the fall of the islands. There were two axes which could be followed. One was straight in over the beaches to the east; these were obstructed with anti-tank and anti-personnel mines (waterproof plastic types) as well as wire, and pebble-filled oil drums. The kelp itself was a useful barrier at many points. The second axis, most favoured in that it offered good landing sites close to the capital, was north and east to Stanley from the Fitzroy inlets on the south coast. Working on this anticipation of enemy aims, the garrison laid minefields to block the possible routes inland. They also held back stocks of mines which were later used to thicken up local defences, and to block ground not otherwise covered. A rough total of 12,000 mines has been reported.

It is an ancient military axiom that he who defends everything ends up defending nothing. Gen. Mario Benjamin Menéndez, the governor and

Royal Marines dug in to cover the San Carlos beachhead; the GPMG is mounted on a sustained fire tripod, although its butt has not been removed as is normal in the SF role. Two boxes of ammunition are stowed as part of the parapet. Under the threat of shellfire, overhead cover is taken seriously, but the machine gunner clearly maintains a fairly optimistic attitude: sharper prints of this picture show a Snoopy mascot attached to his sights! (MoD)

garrison commander, clearly made an effort not to fall into this error. He was assisted in his planning by an intelligence brief prepared in Buenos Aires by Gen. de Bda. Alfredo Sotero, Jefe II/Inteligencia. Fifteen copies of this secret brief were prepared, copies 02 to 13 being sent to the Military Governor of the Malvinas. This secret document contained a mix of information. At the back were pictures of ships and equipment likely to be in the Task Force, with technical details. There was more interesting material at the beginning, however.

The role and structure of special forces were explained, as well as the structure of conventional forces; moreover, between pages 5 and 14 the intelligence officers looked at British options. The two options examined were the direct attack on Stanley, against which Menéndez was to prepare; and the less obvious choice of a landing in a remote area which would provide a base for building up pressure on the Argentine garrison.

Some of the 1,200-odd Argentine prisoners taken at Goose Green are marched off to the 'cage', 29 May; their winter parkas, made in Israel, gave inferior protection to the range of layered clothing worn by the Task Force, and some probably came from northern areas and so had great difficulty acclimatising to the freezing Falklands winter. (MoD)

The conclusions drawn by Sotero's staff were that the main threat was from night attacks; and that helicopters, the key to mobility, were therefore a priority target. They were able to say (on 17 April) that the helicopters would be carried aboard a container ship. They felt that the direct assault option would be too costly in lives; and that the indirect approach would be too slow, as the USA and USSR would put a stop to the fighting by political pressure. However, their assessment of the pre-landing operations was entirely correct:

'Amphibious reconnaissance by the SBS landed from one or more submarines ahead of the main body of the Task Force.

'Isolation of the zone selected for the amphibious assault by the Task Force, and establishment of air superiority over the zone.

'Clearing of any minefields laid on the stretch of coast selected for the landing.

'Final reconnaissance by the SBS and eventually by the SAS.

'Special operations by members of the SBS and SAS, especially on the night before the principal amphibious landing.'

Having blocked the likely routes around Stanley, Menéndez covered the beaches and high ground with OPs which could report movement and landings. Larger settlements like Pebble Island, and Fox Bay on West Falkland, received their own self-contained garrisons. The spine of high ground, running from San Carlos through Mt. Usborne, Wickham Heights, and eastwards to Mts. Challenger and Kent was picketed with OPs; although the men dug in on the high ground (only 705m at its highest) were not artillery spotters, they were to do their job effectively, and had good radio communications with Stanley. When they saw major movement or landings they would call in, and the mobile reserve could be heli-lifted in to seal off a landing and launch a counter-attack.

On the Falkland Islands the population was having to live with occupation. To confirm his standing, Gen. Galtieri flew into Stanley to swear in Gen. Menéndez as governor. To the delight of the locals and the horror of Argentine soldiers the flag, straining in the winter wind, was suddenly tumbled to the mud as the flag pole snapped—just at the moment when Menéndez was taking his oath.

At first the Argentine soldiers tried to make friendly contact with the civilians; but the true character of the Argentine regime was revealed when the head of the local police was replaced by an Argentine intelligence officer named Maj. Patricio Dowling. Dowling—part Irish, part Argentine, and nicknamed 'the Gauleiter' because of his Alsatian dogs and 'cold, creepy manner'—revealed that Buenos Aires had some 500 dossiers on inhabitants of the islands.

There was, however, a lighter note to the occupation. As part of their inept 'hearts and minds' programme the Argentines offered the islanders television sets on which they would be able to watch the World Cup, for a modest down-payment of £10 each and easy terms thereafter. The 'kelpers' still have their TVs, with 140 more instalment payments to go—but the debt collector has been shipped home . . .

South Georgia and Pebble Island

The wastes of South Georgia could never be described as 'occupied' by the small Argentine garrisons at Leith and Grytviken, commanded by the sinister Lt.Cdr. Alfredo Astiz; the British Antarctic Survey party were still at large, as was a two-girl TV team who happened to be making a documentary on wildlife at the time. Indications that the Task Force appeared to be detaching elements towards South Georgia led to the garrison's reinforcement by another platoon of Marines, shipped in by the submarine *Santa Fé*. Before they arrived British troops had already landed.

It is unclear who was first ashore: the SAS, SBS, or Royal Marines. One Marine was certainly with the TV team at one point, since the girls filmed him teaching them to handle a 9mm pistol. He may have come in via HMS *Endurance*, which was cruising in the area acting as a communications link. Otherwise the first recorded landing was on 21 April, by 15 men of Mountain Troop, D Sqn., 22

SAS Regiment, on the Fortuna Glacier. Tasked with reconnoitring the enemy garrison, they found conditions on the glacier impossible; 100mph winds swept away their shelters, and 'environmental casualties' were imminent. The Wessex 5 helicopter sent to extract them from RFA *Tidespring* crashed on take-off from the glacier in appalling 'white-out' conditions; so did the second Wessex which attempted the mission. Eventually the Wessex 3 from HMS *Antrim*, flown by Lt.Cdr. Ian Stanley on his seventh mission in two days, managed to lift out the SAS and the stranded aircrew—a gross overload of 17 passengers—in a feat of airmanship which earned Lt.Cdr. Stanley the DSO. Within hours another team was ready to land, this time using Gemini inflatable assault boats.

The 30kw (40hp) outboard engines of the Geminis are temperamental even under training

Cheerful soldiers of 2 Para after the enemy surrender at Goose Green. Note new fibre helmets, with and without camouflage; and first field dressings taped to webbing, along with smoke grenades. (MoD)

conditions, as the author has discovered; and this time they turned nasty. Fifteen men of 2 SBS and Boat Troop, D Sqn., 22 SAS Regt. set out in five boats. Almost as soon as the first was launched its engine failed, and three men were swept away into the Antarctic night. A second suffered the same fate. (One crew were recovered by helicopter, and the other made a landing, waiting five days before switching on their Sarbe beacon in case they jeopardised the operation.) The other boats landed at Grass Island and set up OPs; the garrison did not appear alert.

The events that led to the recapture of the island were an excellent example of the combination of good luck and judgement that is needed in war. On Sunday 25 April naval helicopters spotted the submarine *Santa Fé* leaving the island after delivering reinforcements. Depth-charged on the surface and badly damaged, she was forced to turn back for Grytviken, and was then strafed with gunfire and AS.12 missiles by *Endurance*'s Wasp and forced to beach.

The original plan envisaged a set-piece landing by M Coy., 42 Cdo; however, the SAS squadron commander on board HMS *Antrim* urged that the land forces should seize the opportunity presented by the confusion of the attack on *Santa Fé*, and go for an immediate landing. By mid-afternoon 30 SAS men and Maj. Sheridan, second in command of 42 Cdo., were ashore; followed up by men of M Coy., they moved the three miles to Grytviken, whose garrison were under observation by a Naval Gunfire Support Forward Observer from 148 Bty.RA, who specialise in this task. The NGSFO called down the first of what would total 6,700 rounds of NGS by the end of the Falklands campaign. Since the emphasis at this stage was on limiting casualties, he did not bring down fire any closer than 800m from identified positions: the bombardment was a demonstration of superior firepower, falling in a controlled pattern which could have left the enemy in no doubt that the Royal Navy could have hit them if it had wanted to.

The defenders' morale took a further knock when the SAS appeared on the enemy position to negotiate their surrender: the Argentine officer protested 'You have just run through a minefield!' Presumably located by watching the area avoided by the enemy as they moved around, the mines may have been lifted, or the safe lane observed and noted, during a previous close reconnaissance of the position.

The enemy at Grytviken were 'bounced' into surrendering by the SAS, who proceeded to run the Union flag up the pole; after refusing a radio invitation to surrender, the 16 men at Leith were persuaded to do so without a fight by a personal visit from the SAS and Marines the following day. The British forces ashore were initially outnumbered by the garrison, which was subsequently found to total 156 Marines and Navy personnel, and 38 civilians.

In view of the earlier Argentine repatriation of the Royal Marines captured on 2/3 April, it was decided to send the Argentine prisoners home via Montevideo. The slightly Renaissance quality of the whole episode was reinforced when the captain of *Santa Fé* and Lt. Cdr. Astiz were dined aboard one of the British warships. In Argentina the response to the defeat was not to ascribe it to guile and superior firepower—as had Astiz in the surrender document he signed aboard HMS *Plymouth*—but simply to deny it had happened, and to claim that their 'lizard commandos' were still in action for days afterwards. There were a few minor casualties on the Argentine side, one submarine crewman losing

Men of Support Coy., 1/7th Gurkha Rifles with a captured enemy twin 20mm AA cannon near Goose Green; some of these weapons were pressed into British service. The exposed position of this gun is odd, given the excellence of many enemy positions. (Paul Haley, 'Soldier' Magazine)

2 June: Guardsmen of 5 Inf.Bde. come ashore at San Carlos under the watchful eye of an AA sentry with a short-barrel Browning M2 .50cal. machine gun. His CEFO includes the lightweight pick; and he is sitting on a rucksack of civilian origin. (Paul Haley, 'Soldier' Magazine)

a leg; and a sailor was unfortunately shot dead in error while the *Santa Fé* was being moved under supervision—an unhappy end to an operation that seemed barely credible, since not one man had been killed in action. The Ministry of Defence were at pains to explain that although the Argentine prisoners were treated according to the Geneva Convention, this did not mean that Britain and the Argentine were 'at war'.

The Spanish Press later revealed that Astiz was an officer active in the 'Dirty War' waged by the Junta in the mid-1970s against internal opposition; one source described him as 'a senior torturer'. The Swedish and French governments expressed a desire to interview him in connection with the disappearance of their nationals in Argentina; these were, respectively, a 17 year-old girl shot in the back and driven away in a car, never to be seen again, and a pair of elderly nuns engaged in medical work. Though briefly held in the UK, Astiz was deported to Montevideo (where, intriguingly, he is reported to have disappeared) when it was established that there was no provision of the Geneva Convention under which he could be questioned against his will by authorities of a third party.

Pebble Island

The raid on Pebble Island on 14 May seemed almost an echo from another war, so reminiscent was it of SAS operations around the Mediterranean in the Second World War.

Why was this tiny community on the northern edge of West Falkland attacked? Firstly, and we believe most importantly, there was an Argentine mobile radar installation there which represented a serious threat to the already-planned landings by the Task Force at San Carlos across the northern end of Falkland Sound. Secondly, the air strip also boasted a detachment of Pucará ground attack aircraft which represented a threat to the landings; and the destruction of these, useful in itself, would 'cover' the destruction of the radar installation, which might otherwise point too clearly to imminent major movement in the area. Pebble Island was also a staging post for C-130 flights from

A Sea King lifts heavy equipment in the background as Guardsmen of 5 Bde. move inland through comrades digging in. (Paul Haley, 'Soldier' Magazine)

the Argentine mainland, whose cargo could be off-loaded there for onward shipment by smaller aircraft or the small ships which operated around the coasts. A cynic might also suggest that there was a need for good news after the loss of HMS *Sheffield*; despite the claim that the Task Force had a free hand, there were moments when it seemed as if the Cabinet was asking them to deliver some good news.

On the night of 11 May eight SAS men—two 'sticks'—had landed on West Falkland opposite Pebble Island, and on the 13th they crossed to establish OPs on the rolling ground directly east of the objective. On the night of 14/15 May they marked a landing zone for helicopters to land 45 men and a naval gunfire expert on the island. The SAS are quick to claim that the NGSFO was the first man ashore. The party was split into an assault group and a cover party, the former to attack the targets and the latter to keep the garrison occupied. The landing was late, and a night march across the island left only half an hour for the attack; for this reason a plan to contact the civilians in the little community was abandoned.

Automatic fire from the covering party, and 4.5in. shells called in at a rate of one every two seconds by the NGSFO, kept many of the enemy in their trenches. The demolition men would have carried in their rucksacks handy-sized charges of plastic explosive, which is both stable and waterproof, with short lengths of safety fuse to allow them time to withdraw. They probably placed all their charges in the cockpits of the Pucarás, to destroy the instruments and to prevent the cannibalisation of one aircraft to repair another. In all they destroyed six Pucarás, a Short Skyvan and five other light aircraft (variously reported as being Puma helicopters or Aermacchis), as well as the radar set and an ammunition dump.

During the withdrawal they were attacked by the Argentine garrison, but this interference ended when the officer who was urging his men forward was spotted and shot. The only British casualties were two men slightly wounded.

Apart from its material effects, the raid was useful in that it worried the Argentine garrisons, and gave them a pattern to expect when more raids took place—a situation which would be exploited during the landings at San Carlos. Dates are not available, but it is known that SAS reconnaissance parties landed during the campaign at Weddell, Port

Stephen, Fox Bay, Chartres, Dunnose Head, Port Howard, Warrah House, Mt. Robinson, Mt. Rosalie, and Byron Heights, all on West Falkland; at Carcass Island, Keppel Island, Sea Lion Island and Lively Island; and, on East Falkland, in the Middle Bay area*, San Carlos, Camilla House*, Douglas, Teal Inlet, Rincon Grande, Port Louis, Diamond Mt., Kydney Island, Mt. Low*, Mt. Kent* and Stanley*(* = contact with the enemy).

A Scimitar of the Blues and Royals, complete with a neat 'basha' for the crew, in position at Bluff Cove. The 30mm Rarden cannon proved effective in the infantry support role. The 'CVR(T)30' Scimitar has a ground pressure of only .35kg per square inch, giving excellent floatation on the soft ground encountered along the northern axis of advance on East Falkland. The passive night vision equipment for commander, gunner and driver came in extremely useful during the final night battles before Stanley. (Paul Haley, 'Soldier' Magazine)

San Carlos and After

The landings on the Falklands began with a disaster on the night of 18 May when a Sea King helicopter ferrying men of 22 SAS Regt. from a briefing lost power on take-off and crashed in the sea—apparently as a result of birdstrike. In the crash 19 men of this small and hand-picked unit were lost; all casualties are tragic, but these were men of exceptional skills.

As the main landing force approached the beaches at San Carlos, the guides who had been ashore since 1 May moved down to mark the landing sites, having checked the area for mines and enemy troops. As part of the deception plan, which involved naval shelling of targets near Bluff Cove and Fitzroy, the SAS put in a major raid on the garrison at Darwin and Goose Green; this was both to mislead enemy intelligence officers as to British intentions, and to keep the garrisons tied up and unable to intervene at San Carlos. About 40 SAS men made a night approach march—later described by one trooper as 'the toughest hike I've ever done with the SAS'—laden with a mix of weapons which were to be used to give the impression of a full battalion attack. The attack achieved all it set out to do: automatic fire, mortar bombs and anti-tank missiles kept the Argentine forces quiet. The 80-lb. loads carried by each man on the outward leg were considerably lightened by the time they withdrew. It is probable that a number of the other raids listed above also occurred on this night, 20/21 May.

Back at San Carlos, the LCMs were moving

Gurkhas prepare to take off from Darwin to clear enemy OPs in the hills, 5 June. Four soldiers rode in each Scout, with feet braced on the skid. (Paul Haley, 'Soldier' Magazine)

through the darkness from HMS *Intrepid* and *Fearless* while the guns of the frigates and destroyers began to soften up targets ashore. On Fanning Head a troop of Argentines were routed by the SBS in a fierce firefight. The LCMs beached, and the Scorpions and Scimitars of the Blues and Royals were first down the ramps to give supporting fire. By 0730 the landings by 40 Cdo. and 2 Para on Blue Beaches 1 and 2 were complete. As the dawn rose 45 Cdo. came ashore at Red Beach in Ajax Bay, and 3 Para, followed by 42 Cdo. in reserve, at Green Beaches 1 and 2 close to San Carlos Settlement.

First casualties were three aircrew of two Gazelle helicopters of 3 Cdo.Bde. Air Squadron shot down by the retreating Argentines, apparently with small arms fire. At least one Argentine Pucará of two or three shot down that day was destroyed by SAS troops—who enjoyed a wider choice of weapons—with a US-made Stinger SAM. That

morning nine 'cold, wet and miserable' enemy prisoners were taken, but ground resistance was brief. The air attacks began in earnest at about 1030 hrs, however, and went on for the next four days with some frequency; it is thought that some enemy aircrew made up to three sorties daily.

As the air defences around San Carlos were improved, the Blowpipes were supplemented by Rapier SAMs, by the CAP Sea Harriers operating well out to sea, and by the 'gun line' of warships with their shipboard systems. The Press aboard the Task Force ships christened San Carlos Water and the northern reaches of Falkland Sound 'Bomb Alley', as the duel between the FAA's Mirages, Daggers and Skyhawks on the one hand, and the Army and Royal Navy SAM and gun crews on the other, grew ever more savage.

For the Rapier crews, operations were unlike anything they had experienced on ranges or simulators. 'The broad, U-shaped valleys meant angle-of-depression problems for the ridge sites, not to mention mist and low cloud; while the valley bottoms severely limited arcs and coverage. Fast jets at 50 feet and travelling at speeds up to and in excess of 500 knots are difficult enough; but add frequent obscuration behind pimples of land, multiple weapons systems all firing at flat trajectories, and the majority of targets being acquired at ranges of 3km or less—and you have something not catered for either in the training films or at the Hebrides.' The new tactics were learned, however, and 40 per cent of the total hits were achieved by 'tail-chaser' missiles.

One lieutenant in 2 Para watched an Argentine pilot switch on his afterburner as a heat-seeking missile nosed towards his aircraft. The massive thermal signature immediately attracted the missile, and the pilot's desperate attempt to achieve escape by speed was his death warrant. The first kills credited to Rapier came when '33 Charlie' of T Bty. (Shah Sujah's Troop), commanded by Sgt. G. J. 'Taff' Morgan, took two Skyhawks.

The problems besetting the SAM crews were similar to those facing the enemy pilots. The shape of San Carlos Water gave incoming aircraft little time to fix a target, whereas the longer approaches along Falkland Sound gave them a clearer run at the Royal Navy's 'gun line'. It was on 23 May that the FAA, after a day's absence, returned in strength. They lost six to eight jets; but succeeded in hitting HMS *Antelope*, and that night her dramatic end lit up the sky and the hills around San Carlos Water.

The forces ashore now comprised all three Royal Marine Commandos and both Para battalions, with a Tactical Brigade Headquarters. Support arms from the invaluable Commando Logistic Regt. were ashore, including the RN Surgical Support Team, which took over the derelict refrigeration plant at Ajax Bay for lack of anything better. They performed miracles in this dank ruin, christened by the piratical Surgeon Cdr. 'Rick' Jolly as 'The Red and Green Life Machine'. For the next few days the main task was to offload stores and ammunition. The loss of *Atlantic Conveyor* on 25 May brutally changed Brig. Julian Thompson's plans for an airmobile advance, with a shock reminiscent of

the ghastly problems thrown in by Directing Staff in the late stages of an exercise. With *Atlantic Conveyor* the Task Force lost stores, RE vehicles, but worst of all, three Chinook and eight Wessex helicopters. It was this loss which obliged the Royal Marines and 3 Para to make their epic 'yomp' along the northern route across East Falkland, a feat of old-fashioned infantry stamina which the enemy had not considered possible.

Orders for the move out from San Carlos were issued on 26 May. It was hardly a 'breakout', since the Argentines had not pressed the beachhead. On the northern route, 3 Para would move to Teal Inlet and 45 Cdo. to Douglas Settlement, with 42 Cdo. in reserve, while 40 Cdo. covered the beachhead; meanwhile 2 Para would move south to Camilla Creek House by 27 May, and would attack Goose Green and Darwin the day after.

Men of 40 Cdo. captured an officer of Argentine Marines on the 27th in the vicinity of San Carlos; later that day an air attack hit a British ammunition dump, and the men around San Carlos had a disturbed night as it continued to explode. Meanwhile enemy OPs on high ground overlooking

81mm mortar crew of 42 Cdo.RM on Mt. Kent. Elements of 42 Cdo. were heli-lifted forward 60km in blizzard conditions, to an LZ on which the SAS and enemy troops were still fighting; and stayed there for six days in temperatures of −12°C, for the first two nights without their sleeping bags. They brought down fire on anything that moved, until finally relieved by 45 Cdo. (MoD)

A Royal Marine, impressively clean-shaven, photographed in blowing snow during the final phase of operations before Stanley. Note first field dressings taped to both SLR butt and belt—all bullets have an exit as well as an entry hole . . . Hoods were only worn up when out of the line and in danger of frostbite: in action they are bad for the hearing, which can be fatal. (Paul Haley, 'Soldier' Magazine)

2 Para's route reported their movement, and Menéndez heli-lifted his reserves from Mt. Challenger down to Goose Green and Darwin. Suddenly the garrison, estimated at 500 men mostly from the Air Force, was swollen to 1,400, good troops, dug in and alert.

Goose Green

The battle which followed lasted throughout the day and night of 28 May. It was fought over very open ground, and against an enemy who withdrew slowly through fixed positions prepared in depth, supported by three 105mm guns, mortars, and 20mm and 35mm twin AA mountings firing in the ground role. The Paras were supported by three 105mm light guns of 8 Bty., 29 Cdo.Regt. RA, which had received a total of 800 tons of ammunition. The British found that the Argentine positions were often linear, as opposed to the all-round positions taught in the British Army; but they chose their ground well, and the trenches had excellent visibility. Machine gun positions sometimes had two guns on sustained fire mounts, positioned to give 360° cover.

It was a line of such trenches that Lt.Col. H. Jones, CO of 2 Para, attacked with men of HQ Coy. when it was holding up the advance of his battalion. His death from wounds did not slacken the impetus of 2 Para's attack; but afterwards there was time to remember an officer who wished, in the best traditions of The Parachute Regiment, to lead from the front. A posthumous award of the Victoria Cross was later announced.

Darwin was taken by mid-morning on the 28th, and Goose Green airfield by the afternoon. The community was surrounded at last light, and the surrender took place on the following morning. During this fighting the Paras found their 81mm mortars most effective against enemy positions; they also brought their Milan anti-tank missiles into action. Designed to penetrate inches of tank armour, and with a range of anything between 25 and 2,000 metres, they proved both accurate and devastating, and became the infantry's own portable artillery.

The enemy surrender at Goose Green was achieved through a remarkable piece of diplomacy by Maj. Chris Keeble, acting CO of 2 Para, and the Spanish-speaking Capt. Rod Bell RM. Keeble sent two captured Argentine NCOs forward under a flag of truce with an appeal to Air Cdre. Wilson Pedrozo, the enemy commander, that as a Catholic he should spare the lives of his men. (It should be noted that, whether through confusion or intent, a flag of truce had not been honoured by the enemy earlier in this engagement.) Keeble's preoccupation with securing an agreement which would safeguard the lives of civilians in the settlement proved to be irrelevant: Pedrozo seemed far more concerned that he should have an opportunity to parade and address his men. Having established their priorities, both sides carried on. The parade, speech, and surrender took place; the Paras released the civilians, who had been locked in a single building for a month—and discovered that they had fought and won a battle at odds of two to one against.

The photographs of long lines of prisoners with one or two guards dotted among the columns, reminiscent of North Africa in the Second World War, were a major boost to British morale; and a blow to the Argentines, who had put in good troops in strength, and lost. The casualty figures showed how the training and motivation of 2 Para had paid off: they had lost 13 killed and 34 wounded, against 250 enemy dead and missing and about 150 wounded. Among the British dead were the crew of a Scout helicopter piloted by Lt. Dick Nunn RM. Blowpipe claimed its first kill for the British with the shooting down of a Pucará by 3 Cdo.Bde. Air Defence Troop.

On 30 May 45 Cdo. reached Douglas, and 3 Para Teal Inlet. They had crossed terrain which is difficult even in good weather, and had done it in hail, rain squalls and icy winds. Leg and ankle injuries were numerous, since the 'going' was either rock, marsh, or rough highland grassland. The men were carrying all their own kit, as well as weapons and ammunition, and some loads weighed 120lb. or even more.

On the same day Maj.Gen. Jeremy Moore RM,

The bleak battlefield west of Stanley, seen from Goat Ridge looking east. Left background. Tumbledown; right background, Mt. William. The terribly exposed terrain, across which the British advanced against enemy who had had weeks to dig in on the dominating features, is shown clearly here. (Paul Haley, 'Soldier' Magazine)

commander of the land forces now that they exceeded one brigade with the arrival of 5 Inf.Bde. at San Carlos, took over the direction of the campaign. The arrival of the Guards and Gurkhas, who had transferred from *QE2* to *Canberra* at South Georgia, was not publicly announced for some days.

On 31 May men of K Coy., 42 Cdo. were helilifted 30km out in advance of the British forward troops to occupy Mt. Kent, a key position outside Stanley. It had already been aggressively reconnoitred by a squadron of 22 SAS Regt., who had harassed the garrison and established that it was not large—the bulk of this unit had been lost at Goose Green and Darwin. The Royal Marines were reinforced by two 81mm mortars and three 105mm light guns. Meanwhile 3 Para moved from Teal Inlet to Estancia House, and then to high ground to the west. The rest of 42 Cdo. were moved up to

Argentine Forces on the Falklands

The initial invasion was carried out by elements of the 2nd Fleet Marine Force, spearhead by special forces of Marine Commando Company 601. The main units involved were the 1st Marine Infantry Brigade, comprising 1st and 2nd Marine Inf.Bns. and a Command and Services Bn.; an Amphibious Reconnaissance Group; the 1st Amphibious Vehicles Bn. (with at least 16 × LVTP-7 and 15 × LARC-5); and anti-tank, heavy mortar and engineer companies. The invasion force seems to have been largely replaced by other units by the time of the British landings. The following tentative order of battle of the garrison at that point is compiled from several sources, which do not always agree on points of detail; the dispositions on the Falklands are from Royal Marines sources, and we are most grateful to Adrian English for his invaluable advice on unit organisation, exact titles, and deployment within the Argentine. The latter is indicated in brackets, where known.

The units identified were drawn mainly from the following formations:

Brigada de Infanteria Mecanizada III (HQ Curuzu-Cuatia, Corrientes)
Brigada de Infanteria Aerotransportada IV (HQ Cordoba)
Brigada de Infanteria Motorizada IX (HQ Comodoro Rivadavia)
Brigada de Infanteria Motorizada X (HQ Palermo, BA)
Brigada de Infanteria Motorizada XI (HQ Bahia Blanca)

There are also tentative reports of the presence of 'mountain troops', which would presumably mean elements of either Brigada de Infanteria Montana V (HQ Tucuman), or VI (HQ Esquel, Chubut). Troops under Army or Corps command are so indicated.

At Stanley (approx. 8,400 men)
Joint Force HQ: General de Brigada M.B. Menéndez
HQ, Brigada de Infanteria Motorizada X: Gen. de Bda. Joffre
Rgt.Inf.Mot.3 'General Belgrano' (Bda.X; La Tablada, BA)
Rgt.Inf.Mot.6 'General Montes' (Bda.X; Mercedes, BA)
Rgt.Inf.Mot.7 'Coronel Conde' (Bda.X; La Plata, BA)
Rgt.Inf.4 (Bda.III; Monte Caseros, Corrientes)
Rgt.Inf.Mot.25 (Bda.IX; Puerto Deseado) (based on Stanley airfield)
Bn.Inf. de Marina 5, and elements Bn.Inf. de Marina 3 (both from 1st Fleet Marine Force, BA)
Cia.Cdo. de M.601
Cia.Cdo. de M.602
Grupo de Artilleria 3 (Bda.III)
(?) Grupo de Artilleria 11 (Bda.XI)
(?) Elements, 1st Marine Field Artillery Bn.
  (Total of at least 30—five batteries—105mm Oto Melara M.1956 pack howitzer, and 3 × French 155mm)
Elements, Agrupacion de Artilleria de Defensa Anti-Aeria 601 (Army troops)
  (Unconfirmed numbers of Rheinmetall twin 20mm and Oerlikon twin 35mm weapons, Skyguard radar prediction)
Elements, Marine AA Artillery Bn. (Tigercat SAM launchers; 1 × Roland SAM, tracked SP)
12 Panhard AML245 H90 armoured cars

  (Unit tentatively identified as *either* Bda.X armoured recce unit Escuadron de Exploracion de Caballeria Blindada 10 'Coronel Isidoro Sanchez', *or* Escn. de Expl. de Cab. Bl. 11, from Bda.XI.)

'601 Engineer Coy.'—could be any one of several units under direct Army command, all bearing designation '601' indicating Army troops.
'181 MP and Intelligence Coy.'—no obvious equivalent appears on Argentine orbat available to us. But 'Intelligence Bn.181' is known to exist, under Army command at Buenos Aires, and if this was a detached company of that unit then the Falkland Islanders have more reason than they know to be grateful to the Task Force; 'Bn.181' has an evil reputation dating from the killings and disappearances among dissident elements during the 'Dirty War' of the mid-1970s.
Air Force, Army Aviation and Air Despatch elements with helicopters (believed 2 × CH-47 Chinook, 9 × Bell UH-1H, 2 × Agusta 109A, several Puma) and Pucará ground attack aircraft.
Naval Aviation detachment, 1st Naval Attack Sqn. (Aermacchi MB.326, 339)

At Goose Green (approx 1,200 men)
Air Force detachment, incl. elements 2nd Attack & Recce Sqn., III Bda. Aerea, with Pucará
Rgt.Inf.Aerotransportada 2 (Bda.IV; Cordoba)
Rgt.Inf.12 (Bda.III; Mercedes, Corrientes)
Artillery half-battery (3 × 105mm)
Element, Agp.Def.AA 601 (4 × twin 20mm & 35mm)

West Falkland: at Port Howard (approx. 800 men)
Element, HQ Bda.de Inf.Mec.III: Gen. de Bda. Parala
Rgt.Inf.5 (Bda.III; Paso de Los Libres, Corrientes)
Element, Cia de Ing.Mot.9 (Bda.IX)

West Falkland: at Fox Bay (approx. 900 men)
Rgt.Inf.Mot.8 (Bda.IX; Comodoro Rivadavia)
Element, Cia. de Ing.Mot.9 (Bda.IX)

At Pebble Island (approx. 120 men)
Air Force detachment with Pucará, confidently identified following SAS raid as from '3rd Attack & Recce Sqn.'; this does not appear on Argentine Air Force orbat available to us, but since approx. 24 Pucarás accounted for on Falklands are easily enough for two full squadrons, it seems likely that this is a newly formed unit of III Bda.Aerea. For full details of enemy air forces, see MAA 135 'Air Forces'.

Much has been made in the popular Press of the difference between 'regular' and 'conscript' units. In fact all units apart from certain small élites are of mixed composition, as is normal in the armies of nations with universal national service laws; young conscripts are posted to all units, serving alongside men nearer the end of their one-year service, and with a cadre of career soldiers and senior ranks. The infantry units posted to the Falklands were brought up to strength by hasty cross-posting from other regiments, and some had a higher proportion of men with very little time in uniform than the normal average of roughly 25 per cent. This hasty transfer of men between regiments goes some way to explain, though not to excuse, the evident confusion in the staff echelons after the surrender at Stanley, when families were unable to discover through official channels whether their sons had even been on the islands, let alone whether they survived. It also recalls the massive over-estimates of troops under his command made by Gen. Menéndez at the time of the surrender.

1: Private, 3rd Bn. Parachute Regt.
2: Brig. Julian Thompson, 3 RM Cdo. Bde.
3: Royal Marine, Naval Party 8901

A

1: Lt.Col. H. Jones, 2nd Bn. Parachute Regt.
2: Sergeant, 2nd Bn. Parachute Regt.
3: Sniper, 2nd Bn. Parachute Regt.

B

1: GPMG, 3rd Bn. Parachute Regt.
2: LMG, Royal Marine Commandos
3: .50 cal.MG, 2nd Bn. Scots Guards

C

1: Rapier SAM
2: Blowpipe SAM
3: 81mm mortar, 1st Bn. Welsh Guards
4: Milan, 1st Bn., 7th Gurkha Rifles

D

1: Sergeant, RMP
2: Piper, 1st Bn., 7th Gurkha Rifles

E

1: Maj.Gen. Jeremy Moore, RM
2: Surgeon Commander, RN, 3 RM Cdo.Bde.
3: Corporal, 1st Bn., 7th Gurkha Rifles
4: Parachute Regt.
5: CW cap

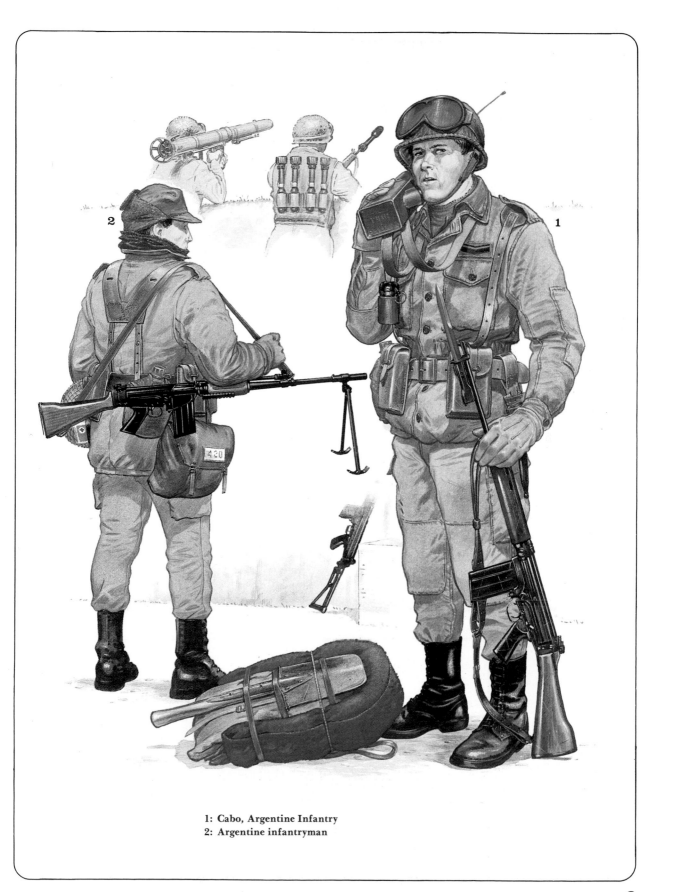

1: Cabo, Argentine Infantry
2: Argentine infantryman

1: Gen. de Bda. Menendez
2: Cabo 1º, Bn. Inf. de M. 5
3,4: Teniente & Marine, Marine Commandos
5: Commando, M. Cdo. Co. 601

H

reinforce K Coy., consolidating on Mts. Kent and Challenger. The eight AFVs of the Blues and Royals, who had followed the northern route, moved south-east towards Kent and Challenger; they had survived some very hard terrain, and had proved the worth of their design concept.

With the Marines and Paras on Kent and Challenger, a busy time followed while PoWs were moved back from Goose Green and the men and equipment of 5 Bde. were brought forward; one priority was to bring 7, 8 and 79 Btys. of 29 Cdo. Regt. RA forward with 1,000 rounds per gun—a task which stretched the reduced heli-lift capacity. Movement was by air, weather permitting, but the LSLs were also used. The long winter nights gave cover from air attack and observation alike. On 4 June the LSL *Sir Tristram*, and LCMs from HMS *Intrepid*, moved 2nd Scots Guards around the southern coast to the Bluff Cove area. When they landed after their freezing and exhausting journey the Guards were revitalised by a Falklands housewife who opened up her deep-freeze and cooked chops all round.

These landings at Fitzroy had become possible after Maj. John Crosland of 2 Para made a discreet

As 2nd Bn.The Scots Guards dig in on the open ground, and a Wessex lifts away on its tireless shuttle back and forth with more men and supplies, the Gazelle of 5 Bde. commander Brig. Tony Wilson lands on Goat Ridge. Note the modification which sends the exhaust heat upwards, a counter to enemy heat-seeking SAMs, and the rocket pods mounted on the transverse bar through the fuselage. Details will be found in MAA 135, 'Air Forces'. (Paul Haley, 'Soldier' Magazine)

phone-call to Reg Binney, the farm manager at Fitzroy. This call on 3 June established that the Argentines had pulled out the day before. Men of 2 Para were hastily lifted forward by helicopter to secure the area; this coup saved a slow advance to contact, and also saved 5 Bde. from the problem presented by the bridge at Fitzroy, which is hard to bypass.

The Gurkhas of 1/7GR took over at Goose Green from 2 Para; led by their new CO, Lt.Col. David Chaundler, who had made a water jump from a C-130 to join them, the Paras now came under command of 5 Brigade. The Gurkhas made a succession of airborne attacks on suspected enemy positions which had been left behind the forward edge of the battle area. The Press called it 'mopping up'; if the domestic analogy is retained, it was more like a series of sharp squirts of insecticide bringing

Enemy shells fall among 2nd Scots Guards as they dig in below Goat Ridge; the white burst is phosphorus. (Paul Haley, 'Soldier' Magazine)

down troublesome flies. With four men riding each Scout helicopter, the Gurkhas would put in parties of about a dozen men to attack suspected OPs, covered by Gazelles with SNEB rockets. This efficient technique netted an enemy party from West Falkland armed with SAM-7 missiles.

As men and ammunition were being moved up to the perimeter around Stanley by sea and air, patrols were going out nightly to dominate no-man's-land and to examine minefields and defences. The SAS and SBS were active on both East and West Falkland. One journalist watched an SAS 'stick' report the details of a fighting patrol near Stanley, and was impressed by the matter-of-fact phrases preferred by the SAS to the rather more flamboyant 'zapping' and 'wasting' of Paras and Marines: 'Took two, wounded two, killed three.' It is ironic that after their surrender the Argentines were to complain about superior night-fighting aids: it was not the equipment, but rather the men who were in their element by night.

A Harrier strip had now been completed at Port San Carlos—after a delay caused by loss of metal matting on *Atlantic Conveyor*—and aircraft operating from it were now called in against 155mm gun positions which had been shelling 3 Cdo.Bde. troops.

Fitzroy

The cycle of triumph and tragedy which had become the rhythm of 'Corporate' hit a tragically low note on 8 June, when Argentine jets successfully bombed the LSLs *Sir Tristram* and *Sir Galahad* at Fitzroy. Although the former had almost completed off-loading by 1700hrs, large numbers of men from 1st Bn. The Welsh Guards were still aboard *Sir Galahad* when she was hit. In the explosions and raging fire which followed, 41 Welsh Guardsmen and two Sappers died, and another 46 Guardsmen were wounded, some of them very severely; total casualties from the raid were 146, of which 63 died.

As the lifeboats and rafts reached the shore, soldiers waded into the freezing water to assist the survivors. Helicopters flew straight into the blinding smoke-pall above the deck, where ammunition was exploding, to snatch other men off the ship; and used the down-draught of their rotors to push life rafts away from blazing oil on the water. When the casualties had been moved off the beach, somebody made the welcome discovery that lifeboats contain emergency rations, including various high-energy items. That night some soldiers supplemented combat rations with condensed milk and other prizes.

There was a further air raid on the beach that evening, but by now missile batteries and automatic weapons had been set up, and four out of five Skyhawks were reported knocked down. One soldier watched others engage the aircraft with small arms—a technique taught in the British Army since its successful use by the Vietcong. He saw one aircraft start its bombing run, and then: 'You could almost see the pilot thinking "*Oh*, no!" and roll away', as the sky above the bay filled up with red tracer—and with the four unseen ball rounds which accompanied each tracer round. That was one A-4 which did not make it home, although others sank an LCM that day, with the loss of four Marines and two RN ratings.

The Argentine estimates of the losses caused at Fitzroy were greatly inflated, and the Ministry of Defence and the commanders on the spot realised that it would benefit their plans if Menéndez were led to believe that the British capability to launch an attack had been disrupted.

The Final Battles

On 10 June Brig. Thompson gave orders for the capture of Mt. Longdon, Two Sisters, Mt. Harriet and Goat Ridge. Many of these features resemble the Dartmoor Tors: outcrops of rock at the top of long, exposed hillsides, some of them linked by saddles of high ground but—in clear weather—giving the defenders excellent visibility. The troops to be used were 42 Cdo., 45 Cdo., 3 Para, 1st Welsh Guards (one company, with two companies 40 Cdo.), and 2 Para under command and in support.

The men of 3 Para were to assault and capture Mt. Longdon, and 2 Para would move so as to be able to support them. To their south, 45 Cdo. was to take Two Sisters. South again, 1st Welsh Guards with two companies of 40 Cdo. under command would secure a start line for an attack on Mt. Harriet, from which 42 Cdo. would then assault and capture that feature while the composite battalion remained in reserve. Although there was to be no unusual artillery preparation, and the attack was to go in as silently as possible in the initial stages, there was considerable gunfire support laid on for the subsequent stages. Five batteries of 29 Cdo. Regt. RA, two of them in support from 5 Inf.Bde., were supplemented by four RN warships: HMS *Avenger* for 3 Para, *Glamorgan* for 45 Cdo., *Yarmouth* for 42 Cdo., and *Arrow* for an SAS squadron making a simultaneous assault on Murrel Heights. The CO of 29 Cdo.Regt. RA co-ordinated the fire support, and had an 'on call' list of 47

targets. During the fighting on the night of 11/12 June 3,000 rounds would be fired, some on targets 50 metres from the forward friendly positions.

When the fighting was over the announcement through MoD in London spoke of Argentine soldiers being 'surprised in their sleeping bags'. They may have started off like that, but the night was to see heavy fighting on all positions.

On Mt. Longdon, 3 Para fought a fierce battle with the Argentine 7th Inf.Regt., who had dug themselves in among the crags and who used their night snipers very effectively. The capture of the feature cost 3 Para 17 dead and 40 wounded. During this action Sgt. Ian McKay took command of his platoon when his officer had been shot in both legs, and went forward to destroy three Argentine machine gun positions with hand grenades. He received a posthumous VC. On Two Sisters 45 Cdo. were faced by a reinforced company of the 4th Inf. Regt., with .50cal. machine guns in strong positions; 45 Cdo. lost four dead and eight wounded.

The remainder of 4th Inf.Regt. were on Mt. Harriet. The Welsh Guards Recce Platoon 'shot in' a diversionary attack on the west side of the feature using Milan, while 42 Cdo. hooked round to the south and assaulted it from the rear. The Argentines were taken by surprise in this classic infantry attack, and the Royal Marines took their objective for one

Mortar Platoon, 1st/7th Gurkha Rifles take a break after firing all night during the battle for Tumbledown and Mt. William on 13/14 June. They wear olive green rainproofs, CW caps and '43 pattern steel helmets. (Paul Haley, 'Soldier' Magazine)

killed and 13 wounded. During this series of attacks some Argentine soldiers came in to surrender from adjoining positions not under direct attack; the sight of the incoming fire, and the prospect of a similar fate sooner or later, were apparently sufficient to overcome the inadequate leadership of their officers and NCOs and the poor motivation of these conscripted defenders of the 'Malvinas'.

It was while giving NGS to 45 Cdo. in this night battle that HMS *Glamorgan* was hit and damaged by a land-launched Exocet missile.

In the original plan the attack would have been pressed the following night, with 2 Para assaulting Wireless Ridge under command of 3 Cdo.Bde., while 2nd Scots Guards attacked Mt. Tumbledown and the Gurkhas went for Mt. William. In the event the attack was postponed for 24 hours. In the meantime artillery fire was exchanged with the enemy 105mm and 155mm guns around Stanley, and the airport runway was brought under fire.

By this stage in the campaign artillery fire had shown itself to be very effective. Though Argentine soldiers might not be killed in great numbers, the constant pounding of British 105mm shells forced them underground and sapped their morale. Some officers watched their young conscript soldiers reduced to silent immobility by the shelling: 'they were stunned'. During the nights of 10 to 13 June helicopters brought forward over 400 rounds per gun; by the end of the fighting it was reported that some guns were down to six rounds, and that over 2,400 rounds had been fired in the final advance.

The enemy gunners returned this fire, and one Para officer remarked afterwards that 'steady shelling by 155s eventually makes you rather shaky'. He recalled how many non-smokers had taken to tobacco, and not as tentative schoolboy smokers might, but as veteran 40-a-day men. Even 3 Cdo.Bde. HQ was not spared surprises; A-4s dropped retard bombs on its position at Bluff Peak near Mt. Kent, although fortunately there were no casualties. One Marine officer remarked: 'You can get used to shelling, but no man gets used to bombing!'

Patrols were still going out to establish the position of Argentine minefields. These operations require patience, and a quiet courage that makes demands upon even the strongest soldier. The minefield reconnaissance was extremely testing, and one sergeant went out three nights in succession—on the third night on his own, after his first two patrols had suffered casualties.

At 0030hrs on the night of 13/14 June, 2nd Scots Guards put in a diversionary attack on a position 2km south of their main objective on Tumbledown. The attack ran into an enemy platoon and took casualties, but it allowed G Coy. to get a lodgement on the objective.

The Scots Guards attack was part of a Brigade plan including subsequent attacks on Mt. William and Sapper Hill by the 1st/7th Gurkha Rifles and 1st Welsh Guards. The Scots Guards had HMS *Yarmouth* and *Phoebe* on call, and the guns of 4 Field Regt. and 7 Bty., 29 Cdo.Regt. at priority call and under the control of Maj. R. T. Gwynn with 2SG; when they started firing they did not let up for more than three minutes at a time for the next 14 hours. In addition, the 'Jocks' had three mortar platoons and a platoon of Browning .50cal. machine guns in support. The battalion was committed to a three-phase assault consisting of company attacks on different parts of the feature.

As Left Flank Coy. moved forward from the G Coy. position it took casualties from enemy mortars, machine guns and snipers; there was also some shelling of G Coy. and battalion headquarters. Left Flank were caught in a difficult position, with high rocks on each side and only a 50-metre wide valley in front. Capt. W. D. Nicol, the RA FOO with the lead company, brought down heavy fire on the enemy—a task made difficult by the fact that the two sides were only 100 metres apart in pitch darkness. For the gunners there were also the problems of clearing a crest line and co-ordinating illuminating rounds. Left Flank remained pinned down until, following this heavy bombardment, they put in a vigorous company attack and secured their objective by 0820hrs; it was during this action that the Guardsmen made a very effective assault with fixed bayonets, a tactic normally held to be anachronistic in these days but which still has its uses. Afterwards they discovered that their enemy had been the Argentine 5th Marine Infantry Battalion. Scots Guards casualties were nine dead and 41 wounded; enemy casualties were about 100, and the 27 prisoners included the battalion commander.

The Gurkhas were tasked to move round the northern flank of Tumbledown when it had been secured. As they advanced they came under observed artillery fire, suffering ten casualties. Their troubles were increased by reports of a minefield stretching north from Tumbledown, but by great good fortune they passed its southern boundary. While the Gurkhas were moving across their start line the Welsh Guards were advancing in the south, and here they ran into minefields laid to cover this axis, two Marines having their feet blown off. It was slow work feeling a way forward through the minefield in the dark; an RA sergeant working as assistant to the battery commander attached to 1 WG said later that he had never in his life followed so closely in the footsteps of his BC.

By dawn the Gurkhas were on Mt. William, and to the north 2 Para were on Wireless Ridge. Apart from NGS the Paras had enjoyed direct support from the Blues and Royals, the rapid-fire 30mm Rarden cannon of the Scimitar proving very effective. They lost three dead and 11 wounded.

From the newly captured features the British troops, squinting in an icy, snow-laden wind, could

Casevac on the morning of 14 June: 'walking wounded' Scots Guards make their way to a Scout. In fact the Guardsman with the bandaged head was severely injured, and his mates carry his kit. At right, carelessly caught by the camera, a Marine of M & AW Cadre, identified by his M16, only carried by special forces. Other tell-tale indicators, we are told, were the superior Gortex rainproofs worn by some SAS men; and the load-carrying jerkins, similar to the old 1943 Battle Jerkin, worn by some SBS Marines in preference to webbing equipment. (Paul Haley, 'Soldier' Magazine)

see the Argentine soldiers leaving their trenches and streaming back into Stanley. The gunners hastened this retreat, as FOOs watched and corrected the fire on the tiny, stumbling figures showing dark against the white ground. 'It was a most pathetic sight, and one which I never wish to see again', recalled the CO of 4 Field Regt. RA.

It was time for Gen. Moore to use discretion as well as strength. Brig. Thompson called off a cluster-bomb attack on Sapper Hill by Harriers from Ajax Bay when the jets were only three minutes from weapons release. (The Harriers had already used laser-guided bombs against Argentine AA positions with great effect that morning.) Contact had been made with the Argentines through a Spanish-speaking Royal Marines officer, Capt. Rod Bell, who was based on HMS *Fearless*. The word was

9 June, between Bluff Cove and Fitzroy: a 105mm light gun crew of C Sub., 29 'Corunna' Bty., 4 Field Regt.RA prepare to send on its way to Sapper Hill one of the 2,400 rounds fired during the final advance on Stanley. (Paul Haley, 'Soldier' Magazine)

passed via a civilian doctor in Stanley, and a meeting was arranged with Menéndez. White flags began to appear all over Stanley.

The men of 2 Para had reached the race course when they were ordered to halt, much to their chagrin. Troops of J Coy., 42 Cdo. moved through them into the town; it was they who would later enjoy a personal triumph when they ran up a Falklands Islands Union flag on the mast at Government House. It was the flag they had kept ever since the firefight with Argentine Marines on 2 April—these were the men of NP8901, returned via the UK after their repatriation by the Argentines.

The Argentine surrender was not filmed or photographed, in contrast to the Argentine coverage of a victory considerably less hard-won. Even the Instrument of Surrender was a curiously muted document: a simple sheet of typewritten paper. The surrender became effective at 2359hrs Zulu on 14 June, 2059hrs local time. Menéndez made an alteration before signing, crossing out the words 'unconditional' and 'Lafonia' for the sake of his self-respect.

A signal was sent to London via the SAS link with Hereford. In it Maj.Gen. Moore allowed himself a modest flourish for posterity: 'The Falkland Islands are once more under the government desired by their inhabitants. God Save the Queen. Signed: J.J.Moore'.

An Argentine poster torn from a wall in Stanley and brought home by a member of the Task Force

takes the form of a florid passage of blank verse; at one point it contains the lines: '. . . What are these British, anyway? Low-born mercenaries, who do not know what they are fighting for!' In an interview shortly after his victory Gen. Moore answered for his men:

'The basic difference was that they were fighting for the islands; we were fighting for the islanders'.

Conclusion

General Moore was to quote Wellington after Waterloo when he described the victory as a 'near-run thing'. As at Waterloo, the military facts had pointed to a victory for the enemy. In both actions it was the British soldier who won, and his strength of character and belief in what he was fighting for—mostly, the close bond which ties a military unit together—which saw him through.

It is a military axiom that one of the keys to success is selection and maintenance of aim. The aim was to get the Argentine forces off the islands, and the best way to do this was to get to Stanley. In pursuing this aim the Task Force was blessed with a government that did not waver—probably the first one since 1945.

Crucially, the difference was between the officers and soldiers on the two sides. When I asked a young Para officer what he saw as the worst and best features of the enemy, he said without a moment's pause, 'The relationship between the officers and men—neither respected the other'; and then, after a pause for thought, 'They dug good positions'.

This relationship was exemplified when a journalist watched a British battalion commander check the list of his men killed and wounded after an attack. He knew their family backgrounds and characters, their skills, even their favourite sports. General Menéndez did not know how many men were in and around Stanley when he surrendered—he was mistaken by a margin of thousands.

British troops and journalists found to their surprise that the Argentine Army issued two distinctly different ration packs: an assault ration, and a large 'GS' type pack which contained more food, of better quality, extra comforts, and an issue of cigarettes and whisky. When in the field British officers use identical 24-hour ration packs to their men, and if feeding is done centrally it is a tradition that they wait until all their men have been fed before joining the queue. The religious and political tracts stuffed in every Argentine ration pack are unlikely to have made up for the way officers generally 'acquired' the larger pack.

Reports published in Buenos Aires reinforced this impression of deficient leadership. Conscripts were punished by being forced to stand in the open in freezing rain without gloves, boots or headgear; and this punishment was for deserting their posts to go in search of food. No army can allow its men to straggle off looking for food—and no army should oblige them to do so. There were moments when rations did not reach British units on the Falklands, but the men knew that this was not because of a policy of giving them the least, last. The Argentines had food available in Stanley, but it was not brought forward to outlying positions.

The soldiers who invaded the Falklands were capturing an island and an idea; the men who liberated them were less concerned with the country than with the people, and the principle. Conscripts can be good soldiers when they are well led and trained. The poor leadership suffered by most of the Argentines led to fantastic rumours growing among them—such as the story that Gurkhas killed their own wounded and ate their prisoners, and that British special forces were mingling with the defenders dressed in Argentine uniform and speaking perfect Spanish. The military historian hears echoes of the Battle of the Bulge in one Argentine soldier's report that 'There was so much fear we tried to find questions to ask them that an Argentine would know easily, but that an English commando would not know, even if he spoke perfect Spanish'.

In training British officer cadets learn one lesson very early: 'There is no such thing as a bad soldier, only a bad officer'. The relationships between officers and men of both sides in the Falklands campaign, and the results which flowed from them, have borne out this lesson yet again.

Scots Guards bring in Argentine prisoners from Tumbledown; note the bulk of the IWS—individual weapon sight—a passive night vision device. Argentine equivalents were smaller, lighter, and handier. (Paul Haley, 'Soldier' Magazine)

'It's all over!' Jocks of 7 Platoon, G Coy., 2SG hear the news of victory on 14 June. This battle-stained group display an amazing miscellany of clothing and equipment: second right wears the quilted trousers worn under the CW suit; beside him is a soldier—a piper?—in a Glengarry; behind him is the GPMG number with IWS fitted, probably the most effective use for this device. (Paul Haley, 'Soldier' Magazine)

The Plates

(Research by Michael Chappell and Martin Windrow)

The haste with which the British were forced to mount a winter campaign in the South Atlantic led to the use of a variety of combat clothing. Apart from personally-acquired civilian items, surprisingly often seen in photos of the campaign, the main outfits were as follows:

1. Windproof suits. Developed from the Second World War smock and over-trousers popularly associated with the SAS, these suits were worn by men of the RM 3rd Cdo.Bde., 2 and 3 Para, and—presumably—the SAS and RM SBS sections. Identifying features are 'bellows' smock pockets, a yoke seam where the hood is attached, and absence of epaulettes. There are two patterns: the 'RM pattern' with a wire-stiffened hood, and 'epaulettes' for rank slides on the chest and back; and what might be termed the 'SAS pattern', with no rank slide straps and an unstiffened hood. Both have velcro fastening at cuff and ankle. The official nomenclature is 'Arctic windproof combat smock and trousers'. The colour is the usual British DPM camouflage of light green, yellow, light red-brown, and black.

2. 'Cold Weather' (CW) suits of parka and over-trousers, both with quilted liner garments sometimes seen worn exposed—a dark green sleeveless waistcoat and trousers. These were issued to 5th Inf.Bde., and are occasionally seen worn by paratroopers. Identifying features are epaulettes, a stiffened hood, 'patch' pockets on the chest, 'bellows' pockets on the skirt, and a strap-fastened parka cuff. Also in DPM. Note that both the windproof and CW suits have oversize buttons, and 'bellows' pockets on both thighs of the trousers.

Foul-weather clothing—basically, thin rainproofs—appeared in at least three varieties: DPM rainproof smocks and over-trousers (5 Bde.); similar items in olive green (5 Bde.); and a curious olive green waterproof smock which appears to have a white inner lining—reversible?—seen in both the Commandos and the Para battalions. In addition, ponchos were seen being worn from time to time, a most unusual sight in the British Army.

Headgear included at least five varieties of helmet, mostly worn covered by layers of sacking, scrim nets, etc.: the new paratroopers' fibre, the old paratroopers' steel, the 1943 steel, the RAC steel worn by RN and some RM personnel, and the AFV crews' fibre. Pile-lined CW caps in DPM camouflage were widely worn, as were unit berets, DPM field caps, knitted cap-comforters, etc. Where metal badges were worn they were normally dulled.

Footwear included the standard 'boots DMS', the 'Northern Ireland', and an amazing collection of civilian fell boots scattered among the issue Arctic footwear of the Marines. Rubber calf-length 'galoshes' or over-boots were issued in quantity, but a variety of civilian waterproof leggings were also seen. Photos indicate that most troops who made the 'long tab' across the north of East Falkland finished it in standard boots DMS and ankle puttees.

Equipment was basically the issue 1958 pattern in all its variations, but with the addition of a variety of rucksacks. Notable are the olive nylon GS, SAS and Paratroop issues; the webbing 'Bergen'; and a job lot of civilian rucksacks which seem to have been bought up from a well-known chain of sports and working clothes suppliers at short notice, some in most unmilitary colours! A final point is that this campaign did not seem to involve the display of 'festoons' of belted GPMG ammunition, most of which seems to have been carried in pouches or bandoliers.

A1: Private, 3rd Bn. The Parachute Regiment
Apart from the new fibre paratroopers' helmet, this soldier could belong to any battallion or commando which served in the Falklands. He wears the windproof parka and over-trousers, DMS boots and puttees. His equipment is standard '58 Pattern with '44 Pattern waterbottle, NBC gear, and toggle rope; the rucksack is the Para issue, with poncho roll and lightweight shovel attached. His weapon is the standard SLR with Trilux SUIT sight attached. He is a living, aching reminder that in the days of shoulder-fired missiles and massive supporting firepower, wars are still won by the infantryman who can march, dig and shoot better than his enemy.

A2: Brigadier Julian Thompson RM
The commander of 3rd Commando Brigade wears the windproof smock and DPM field cap, '58 Pattern webbing belt and pistol holster. His rank, in black cut-out form, is displayed both on the chest of the smock and—apparently a Royal Marine peculiarity—on the cap front. (Brig. Tony Wilson of 5th Inf.Bde. wore the maroon Para beret with the gold lion cap badge of his rank; and a parachute smock of current pattern with the parachute brevet and the maroon 'DZ patch' of 1 Para on the right sleeve, and the battalion's maroon lanyard at the right shoulder.)

A3: Royal Marine, Naval Party 8901
Cradling his 84mm anti-tank weapon, this 'Booty' wears the temperate climate combat dress of the Royal Marines, in which the tiny garrison was photographed after its capture: green Commando beret with darkened globe-and-laurel badge; DPM combat smock and olive green trousers, DMS boots and puttees; and '58 Pattern fighting order, usually supplemented with drab khaki bandoliers.

B1: Lieutenant-Colonel H. Jones, 2nd Bn. The Parachute Regiment
It is our sincere hope that it will not be felt in poor taste to record in this book the appearance of this gallant officer, as he led his battalion in the attack at Goose Green which cost him his life, but which added an impressive chapter to the record of The Parachute Regiment. An eyewitness reports that Lt.Col. Jones paused to change the magazine of his Sterling SMG before moving on to tackle a further Argentine MG position, and shortly after this was hit twice in the back, dying of his wounds some hours later. We have depicted him wearing the full suit of windproof clothing of 'RM pattern', with his ranking—on the light blue backing of the regiment—on the chest tab. The maroon regimental beret has the dulled cap badge; the equipment is '58 Pattern Combat Equipment Fighting Order (CEFO) with NBC gear.

B2: Sergeant, 2nd Bn. The Parachute Regiment
This NCO, getting off a 'double tap' with his SLR

(from which the Trilux sight has been removed for close quarter fighting, but which retains the sight bracket), wears the standard DPM parachute smock; the windproof parka has been removed and stowed behind his shovel, but he retains the over-trousers. On the right sleeve of the smock is the parachute brevet, above the blue 'DZ patch' of 2 Para, above rank chevrons. The current pattern fibre helmet has a DPM cover; padded black leather 'Northern Ireland' gloves are worn.

B3: Sniper, 2nd Bn. The Parachute Regiment

The Paras, at least, took their snipers to the Falklands, as shown by photographic evidence; this sniper has worked forward of the assault groups, and now settles down to shoot at the target he has stalked.

Though hardly visible, our sniper wears the old steel paratroops' helmet and the home-made sniper smock: a very oversize combat smock stitched all over with yards of scrim and hessian, which is still as excellent a form of camouflage as when first

Marines of 45 Cdo., leaning into the weight of their packs, march into Stanley at the end of the long 'yomp'. Carrying the SLR in this way, with magazine and pistol grip trapped against the belly with both hands and arms braced on pouches, spreads the weight across both forearms. (MoD)

introduced in 1915. The modified No.4 rifle is now designated Sniper Rifle L4A1; the sight Telescope, Sighting, L1A1. The high standard of camouflage is matched by high standards of marksmanship and fieldcraft.

C1: GPMG number, 3rd Bn. The Parachute Regiment

The standard section MG is the General Purpose Machine Gun, 7.62mm, normally issued three per platoon, giving a total of between 50 and 60 per infantry battalion. (In the Falklands 2 Para, at least, had six per platoon.) The paratrooper who wields it wears the regimental beret, and the green–white 'smock, combat, reversible' seen in many photos of the campaign. Under it his DPM parachute smock would bear on the right sleeve the green 'DZ patch' of this battalion. He has the Para rucksack, '58 Pattern CEFO with NBC equipment, and the steel helmet.

C2: LMG number, Royal Marine Commandos

The excellent and much-loved Bren LMG of the Second World War has not entirely disappeared from the British forces. In its modified 7.62mm form, and rechristened 'L4A2', it still has a role as a lighter and handier section weapon than the belt-

fed GPMG, and is issued particularly for tropical service. Photos show that it was used in the Falklands; note that the change to the NATO 7.62mm round caused the adoption of a straight magazine compatible with SLR magazines in place of the old 'banana'. The Marine wears the windproof parka, olive green trousers, and olive green waterproof leggings.

C3: MG number, 2nd Bn. The Scots Guards

The Guardsman wears the khaki Foot Guards beret with dull bronzed 'cap star', and the CW parka suit. His weapon is more interesting then his outfit: the short-barreled .50cal. Browning M2 anti-aircraft conversion, whose sudden resurrection for the Falklands campaign came as something of a surprise, but which by all accounts proved invaluable. Large numbers were bought from the USA in the early 1950s, the intention being to arm all vehicles for AA defence, in the US Army manner. The 1-ton and 3-ton vehicles were modified to mount the .50cal., and the School of Infantry ran courses in the use of the weapon. However, the policy changed; the gun was never issued, and the course was discontinued in the mid-'50s. That the weapons should have been held in store for a quarter of a century is extraordinary— that battalions should have found instructors in its use during the brief period before the landings is even more so! Accounts of the fighting before Stanley suggest that the Browning was issued to a platoon within HQ Company—in this battalion, at least—and that it was used with some effect against Argentine ground positions, as well as adding heavy metal to the curtain of light flak over the landing beaches.

D: Support Weapons

D1: Rapier (British Aerospace)

Designed as a battlefield defence system against supersonic aircraft, Rapier is a land-mobile, air-portable surface-to-air tactical guided missile. The guidance system is semi-automatic command to line of sight. The solid-propellant rocket, with an HE warhead, weighs 143lbs. and is 7ft.4ins. long; its ceiling is approximately 16,400ft., and its speed is believed to be about Mach 2. In the Falklands it was operated by batteries of Light Air Defence Regiments, Royal Artillery, and by the Royal Air

Meanwhile, in the streets of Stanley, Marines of 42 Cdo. pause to fraternise during a house clearing patrol. In the background is the police station, hit by AS.12 missiles fired from a Wessex 5 helicopter flown by Petty Officer Ball the previous week, when it was an enemy command post. (MoD)

Force Regiment. On occasion, when it had recently been 'shaken up' by urgent landing on shore, the crews were unable to 'set up' the complex control systems before the arrival of enemy air strikes; and it proved tricky to operate in a role for which it had never been intended, i.e. firing *downwards* from hilltops at enemy aircraft passing down valley floors or over crowded anchorages at mast height. Overall, however, its performance was very satisfactory, and it is believed to have been responsible for 14 aircraft 'kills'.

D2: Blowpipe (Short Bros.)

This man-portable surface-to-air missile is also operated by elements of LAD Regts., RA, providing close-range defence against aircraft attacking at low altitude—ideally, aircraft coming head-on at the operator. It can acquire targets flying away, but does not have the endurance of 'burn' for a long tail-chase. Guidance is by radio/optical tracking. The solid-propellant rocket

A local boy is given a ride on the Blues and Royals' Samson ARV. (Paul Haley, 'Soldier' Magazine)

has an HE warhead. Blowpipe's weight is 47lbs., its length 4ft. 7ins. An estimated nine aircraft fell to this weapon in the Falklands. Here the operator wears standard CW suit and cap.

D3: 81mm mortar (RARDE)
The 'battalion commander's artillery', the 81mm mortar is highly accurate and capable of a rate of fire of 15rpm. It can throw bombs out to a maximum range of 4,500m (with charges 1 to 6) and 5,660m with charges 7 and 8; these charges refer to supplementary propellant explosive charges clipped to the tail. The HE round weighs 9.7lbs.; alternatives are WP, smoke and illuminating rounds. It is operated by a crew of three, in the specialist mortar platoon of the infantry battalion's support company. It weighs 79lbs. The crewmen are shown here wearing a mixture of rainproof and CW clothing; note Welsh Guards beret.

D3: Milan (Euromissile)
This second-generation wire-guided missile, man-portable and weighing 50lbs., provides the infantry battalion with an anti-tank capability, and replaces the Mobat, etc., recoilless guns. The guidance system is semi-automatic: the operator has only to keep his cross-hairs on the target. The maximum range is 2,000m, and flight time to that range is $12\frac{1}{2}$ seconds. The missile uses solid propellant, and has a hollow charge HE warhead capable of penetrating 352mm of armour plate at an angle of 65°. The Paras, Welsh Guards and 7th Gurkha Rifles, in particular, found the Milan of great value in attacking well-prepared Argentine infantry

positions, against which it proved absolutely devastating. The operator wears the olive green rainproof suit, and the 1943 steel helmet.

E1: Sergeant, Royal Corps of Military Police
Photos suggest that as soon as the Argentine surrender came into effect at Stanley the RMPs of at least one unit's detachment quickly 'smartened up'. Their normal traffic control duties presented few problems, under the circumstances; but the processing of PoWs was a heavy burden indeed . . .

This NCO wears the RMP scarlet beret with bronze cap badge; the DPM combat smock, with a brassard in the same cloth combining a personal parachute brevet, small black-on-green rank chevrons, and the MP patch; olive green polyester overall trousers, which were not a popular item; and over-boot 'galoshes'. The '58 web belt supports the pistol case for the 9mm Browning, a taped-on field dressing, and the S6 respirator pouch.

E2: Piper, 1st Bn., 7th Duke of Edinburgh's Own Gurkha Rifles
Photos show that 1/7GR took their pipers to the Falklands, as did 2SG, whose pipe major followed worthily in the traditions of his predecessors by composing a new piece entitled 'The Crags of Tumbledown' to commemorate the battalion's engagement at that place. The Gurkha piper wears the regiment's Rifle green beret and silver cap badge, and CW smock and over-trousers.

In the background a squad of happy Marines pass in a truck, one of them (based on a figure immortalised by news film) flying a large Union flag from the antenna of his PRC351 radio.

F1: Major-General Jeremy Moore RM
The GOC ground forces of the South Atlantic Task Force had two personal 'trademarks' which were noted from photos and news film: a unique field cap (possibly Norwegian) in faded olive, bearing his rank insignia in black cut-out form; and a small olive green back-pack of civilian origin, which he was still wearing when he ran down the steps of the transport aircraft which flew him home to RAF Brize Norton. Otherwise his outfit was severely orthodox, comprising windproof DPM parka and trousers, and a '58 web belt with pistol holster. Note ranking on DPM chest tab.

F2: Surgeon Commander, Royal Navy Surgical Support Team

Specialists such as medical personnel, engineers, etc., serving alongside the three Royal Marine Commandos wear the cap badge of their parent service or organisation on the green beret which signifies success in the Commando course. The Marines have Royal Navy doctors; and one, Surgeon Commander 'Rick' Jolly RN, became a widely-known 'face' after he had appeared in front of an audience of millions on the TV screen, being interviewed outside the derelict refrigeration plant at Ajax Bay in which the medical team were forced to carry out more than 100 major operations in the days and nights following the landings. Under unavoidable conditions of cold, filth, and danger the teams achieved the remarkable success of 'sending out alive anyone who came in alive'; this, with two unexploded Argentine bombs lodged in the building only feet from the operating tables, and under intermittent air attack which blew up an ammunition dump nearby, and obliged the surgeons to operate wearing steel helmets. The officer wears his Royal Navy cap badge on the Commando beret, and his commander's shoulder ranking in gold, divided by the surgeon's red stripes, on the front tab of the windproof parka.

F3: Corporal, 1st Bn., 7th Duke of Edinburgh's Own Gurkha Rifles

The Gurkha wears the DPM combat smock with the similarly patterned over-trousers of the CW suit, a knitted cap comforter, 'galoshes', and 'NI gloves'. The '58 CEFO equipment includes the lightweight pick, and a Gurkha peculiarity: a DPM cover for the kukri knife at the right hip. Rank chevrons are worn on the right sleeve only, in the traditional Rifles colours of black on green common to all Gurkha units. The black shoulder patches are indicators of the battalion (triangle, right shoulder) and company (circle, 'C' Coy., left shoulder); others are a square for 'B' Coy., a cross for HQ, etc.

F4 is a detail view of the maroon beret of the two battalions of The Parachute Regiment which served in the Falklands; *F5*, the pile-lined, DPM cloth CW cap. The cap badges of the major units which served in the campaign are presented against a narrow backing of their beret colours: *left, top to bottom:* Royal Marines, Parachute Regiment, Welsh Guards, Blues & Royals (on midnight blue); *right, top to bottom:* 22 SAS Regiment, Royal Artillery (on midnight blue), Scots Guards, 7th Gurkha Rifles; *centre,* Army Air Corps. Only space prevents us from including the badges of those supporting units and organisations whose personnel faced the same dangers, and without whose efforts the Task Force would have failed.

G1: Cabo, Argentine infantry

This junior NCO is identified by the thin-above-thick shallow chevrons worn in black above the left breast pocket. Other insignia were one thick chevron (Dragoneante, private); two thin above one thick (Cabo 1°, senior corporal); one thin above two thick (Sargento, sergeant); and one thin bar above one thick bar (Sargento 1°, senior sergeant).

Unit and formation insignia do not seem to have been worn on combat clothing by the vast majority of troops. One prisoner photo shows a small group at Stanley wearing on the left shoulder a square white patch with an unidentifiable device, but these may not even be Army personnel. One, out of several score colour photos in the Argentine Press examined while preparing this book, seems to show men wearing in the same position a mid-green shield shape. On service dress the infantry units wear such a patch, edged gold and with gold crossed rifles in the centre; the photo referred to showed no gold, though it was of poor quality and if a black field version of the insignia was worn it might not have shown up—but this is pure speculation. On the padded parka (Plate H2) a very few troops wore

Some of the enemy Panhard armoured cars, which seem to have remained parked in the street near Stanley waterfront throughout the battle. Foreground, the RA badge on a green beret identifies a gunner of 29 Cdo.Regt., Royal Artillery; background, one of 3 Cdo.Bde.'s Sno-Cat tracked vehicles. (Paul Haley, 'Soldier' Magazine)

With an expressive gesture of disgust, an Argentine prisoner hurls down his rifle. The faces of his comrades tell their own story. (MoD)

a small rectangular patch of the Argentine tricolour flag mid-way between left shoulder and elbow.

The US steel helmet is fitted with one of two identified camouflage covers, this one in a streaky 'fernleaf' pattern of drab green and brown over ochre. The goggles, almost universally worn, were sometimes clear but usually had amber or pink lenses—an aid to acquiring night vision at dusk? The field dressing was normally worn under the goggle strap at the rear; figure G2, whose slung helmet has the more usual string netting, displays the common first field dressing, in white with a blue panel and a red cross in the corner.

The olive drab fatigues have exposed buttons; many jackets did not have shoulder straps. High black combat boots were universal. The equipment harness was usually in this grey-green painted leather; most riflemen wore two pouches, a bayonet frogged on the left hip, a canteen in a simple olive cloth cover on the rear (usually olive plastic, sometimes the old aluminium US type), and a small pack on the right hip. This had a 'window' for name and number—see G2—and may have held field rations, respirator and NBC kit. The wash-leather gloves were widely issued. The grenade is unidentified but may be Italian. The 'prong' bayonet shown here only fitted the solid-butt version of the FN rifle—the more common folding-butt type is shown in the background. There was some use of the old US 'walkie-talkie' radio.

G2: Argentine infantryman
Some troops wore the US M.56 combat jacket, identifiable by its fly front and shoulder straps. The field cap with pile-lined flaps was common, as was

the knitted toque worn round face and neck. Men carrying the heavy-barrel FN/FAL with bipod, as the section light machine gun, usually wore four or even six pouches around the belt. The belt was sometimes brown, as here. The light 'assault pack' in the foreground attached to the slits in the rear of the shoulder harness; it seems to be a folded shelter-half strapped up with a blanket, and the spade—often the old German Wehrmacht type—was thrust under the straps. A frequent alternative was a horse-shoe blanket roll round the body. In the background are men with the US 3.5in. rocket launcher, fitted with a folding bipod; and a carrying vest for rifle grenade rounds, with four across the back and one each side of the chest.

H1: General de Brigada Mario Benjamin Menéndez
The Argentine commander of the 'Islas Malvinas' wears a stiffened olive field cap with a small enamel cockade in the national colours of pale blue and white. His field jacket, similar to that of his men but of better quality, bears gold general officer's leaves on both collar points. This is exposed in the open neck of a type of drab tan quilted, hooded jacket with knit cuffs seen in photos of some Argentine officers. He wears wash-leather gloves, and carries a helmet with the 'fernleaf' camouflage cover held by a narrow black band. The jacket has flapped side pockets; and on the left breast is a cloth strip bearing his rank insignia—a single gold 'sun' of elaborate design, embroidered on a red felt disc.

H2: Cabo Primero, Bn.Inf. de Marina 5
The standard protective clothing throughout the garrison was this padded, hooded parka with a zipped front covered by a snap-fastened fly, and knitted cuffs. The red rank chevrons are speculative; a few photos definitely show red instead of the usual black, but we have been unable to find a photo tying this feature in with other identified unit features. Since the chevrons worn on the Marine service uniform are red, we show them, tentatively, on this Marine figure. The Marine beret, in blue-grey, and the gold badge of crossed cannons and anchor with the Argentine national crest superimposed, are shown in photos. For some unexplained reason some personnel wore it pulled right, but most pulled it to the left as illustrated.

Equipment is otherwise as for the infantry. The

folding-stock FN rifle has a grenade in place, and another is slung on the harness; the red tabs are probably a safety feature removed before firing. Note drab khaki bandolier.

H3 & H4: *Teniente and enlisted man, Marine Commandos*

Two companies are known to have served on the Falklands, numbered 601 (the normal code for Army troops) and 602. The first is a permanent unit, trained to US Ranger standards; the second is thought to have been a newly-raised company assembled for the campaign from men who had qualified as commandos but were then serving with other units. A unit commander is mentioned in the enemy Press, Lt.Col. Ali Mohamed Seineldin ('Turco'), but whether he commanded both companies collectively is not certain. Pre-war photos from Argentina show this camouflage uniform—similar but not identical to British pattern—worn with a dark green beret. Photos from the Falklands during the campaign show the uniform as illustrated here. Camouflage clothing is only worn by these special forces, making them easy to identify on the battlefield.

The officer wears a rank patch on his left breast pocket, as is normal throughout the land forces. The insignia of this rank are one silver and one gold star. Other ranks wear one silver (Alferez, ensign); three silver (Capitan, captain); and one, two and three more elaborate gold 'suns' for the field ranks. The photo we copy in this plate shows a moulded rubber/plastic composition version of the officers' parachute brevet, in yellow, blue and white. Leather equipment is light brown. Both Browning 9mm and Colt .45 pistols were used by the Argentines.

The soldier wears the same uniform, with a combat jerkin in place of equipment harness. This has two grenade pockets high on the chest, with elasticated loops above; below these are two magazine pockets on each side, vertically arranged; and a small pack is built into the rear of the jerkin. The archaic sword-bayonet is incompatible with the FN rifle, but was definitely carried by at least some of these troops.

The Commandos were among the few troops to distinguish themselves. Late in May, during the advance across the island, an OP of 3 Cdo.Bde.'s Mountain and Arctic Warfare cadre (an élite sub-unit) spotted a helicopter-inserted team of 16 men of Argentine Marine Commando Company 602 operating from a building known as Top Malo House near Mt. Simon. As Harrier strikes were not available, they 'took out' the enemy in a classic infantry attack. Nineteen Royal Marines attacked the 16 Argentine Marines, driving them out of the cover of the house with 66mm rockets and then engaging them in the open. The result was three dead, seven wounded and six un-wounded prisoners, for British casualties of three wounded.

H5: *Argentine Marine Commando, Stanley, 2 April*

Sources differ over whether the spearhead of the invasion was provided by 601 or 602 Company of this organisation; the former seems more likely. Much photographed during the searching of the men of NP8901, the men of the first sub-units to attack key points wore this outfit and a set of webbing quite different from the normal issue, resembling US and French models. Magazines for the silenced Sterling 9mm SMG were carried in double leather pouches painted grey-green, but brown pistol holsters were worn. Note goggles hanging round neck.

Persistent rumours that British troops met in battle 'US mercenaries' probably sprang from incidents when Commandos made this claim in the (apparently mistaken) belief that it would save their lives in the heat of action. Enquiries in US

In the sea of discarded and rapidly rusting enemy weapons, one FN displays the kind of religious postcard issued in Argentine ration packs. Many of the troops wore rosaries pinned to their combat jackets. (Paul Haley, 'Soldier' Magazine)

mercenary circles fail to produce any corroboration for an inherently unlikely story. American-trained, some of the Commandos probably speak American-accented English; some certainly wear the 'different equipment' mentioned by British witnesses to some of these incidents: see H4 and above.

Notes sur les planches en couleur

A1: Si l'on fait abstraction du nouveau casque 'fibre' de parachutiste, on pourrait être en présence d'un soldat de toute unité quelconque du corps expéditionnaire. Parka coupe-vent et couvre-pantalon; équipement individuel modèle 58; bidon modèle 44; nouveau sac à dos 'Nylon' avec pelle et rouleau poncho; fusil SLR avec appareil de pointage Trilux. Le poids total, y compris les munitions et armes supplémentaires pourrait dépasser 110 lbs (50 kgs.). **A2:** L'insigne de grade à l'avant de la casquette est particulière aux Royal Marine; notez également la patte pour insigne de grade à l'avant du parka coupe-vent, avec répétition à l'arrière. **A3:** Les membres de la garnison Marine originale continuaient à porter des vêtements d'été en avril. Vareuse DPM, pantalon vert, avec béret vert RM et badge obscurcie. Il tient en mains une arme antichar de 84mm avec laquelle il a endommagé le navire de guerre argentin 'Granville'.

B1: Parka coupe-vent avec insigne à patte indiquant le grade sur fond bleu pale, couleur du régiment. Béret du régiment. **B2:** Casque 'fibre' avec couverture en toile pour camouflage; blouson de parachutiste, couvre-pantalon coupe-vent, parka coupe-vent enlevé et suspendu au paquetage. Bras droit seulement: brevet de parachutiste, au-dessus de la pièce bleue indiquant le bataillon, au-dessus des chevrons indiquant le grade. **B3:** Fusil Lee-Enfield .303 No. 4 converti pour tireur d'élite embusqué; casque en acier couvert d'un camouflage abondant; blouse de combat surdimensionnée, bardée de toile de sac, chiffons etc cousus partout.

C1: Trois GPMG par peleton. Blouse de combat imperméable, verte, à doublure blanche distribuée à certains combattants. **C2:** Fusil-mitrailleur Bren modifié en calibre 7,62mm continuant à être porté parfois. Le Marine porte un parka coupe-vent, un pantalon vert olive, des guêtres civiles, imperméables. **C3:** Béret kaki des Foot Guards, 'Parka CW' et pantalons. Stocks de Browning M2, .50 cal., à canon court, distribués à la hâte pour une protection DCA supplémentaire. Ils peuvent également être utilisés contre les tranchées ennemies lors de l'assaut final.

D1: Utilisé par les unités de DCA de la Royal Artillery; le missile atteint la vitesse Mach 2; il peut s'élever jusqu'à une altitude de 16,400 pieds (5,200m). **D2:** Utilisé dans les deux camps durant cette guerre, Blowpipe, appartenant également à l'armement de la Royal Artillery, est conçu pour tirer sur un aéronef arrivant de front vers l'opérateur plutôt que pour un tir 'poursuite'. **D3:** 'L'artillerie du bataillon d'infanterie, utilisée par la section de mortiers de la compagnie d'armes d'appui du bataillon. Les servants portent des vêtements imperméables, pantalons 'CW' et casquette 'CW', béret des Welsh Guards. **D4:** Missile antichar utilisé avec un effet dévastateur par les bataillons d'infanterie contre des tranchées ennemies.

E1: Béret écarlate du RMP; la combinaison de combat constituant une dotation standard comporte un brassard avec brevet de parachutiste (ce qui indique qu'il s'agit sans doute d'un combattant d'un détachement RMP auprès d'un bataillon aéroporté) au-dessus des chevrons indiquant le grade, et la pièce 'MP'. Caoutchoucs imperméables portées par dessus les chaussures par de nombreux combattants. **E2:** Tous les Gurkhas portent un béret vert foncé, et des autres insignes aux couleurs du Rifle regiment.

F1: Maj.Gen. Moore des Royal Marines portait une casquette d'origine norvégienne avec son insigne de grade à l'avant. **F2:** Les médecins des unités de Marines sont de la Royal Navy; notez l'insigne de la Royal Navy sur le béret vert indiquant qu'il a suivi avec succès un stage de commandos; et l'insigne de grade d'officier chirurgien sur la patte avant du parka coupe-vent. **F3:** Blouse de combat DPM standard, couvre-pantalon coupe-vent, caoutchoucs, 'cap comforter' tricoté, et 'gants d'Irlande du Nord' capitonné. La pièce à triangle noir indique le bataillon; l'autre épaule arbore le symbole distinctif de la compagnie: cercle = Compagnie C; carré = Compagnie B etc. Notez qu'il porte une couverture de toile camouflante sur la gaine du couteau kukri. **F4:** Béret du Parachute Regiment. **F5:** Casquette 'CW': Cold Weather (temps froid). Badges de béret des unités en question représentés sur le fond étroit des couleurs de leurs bérets. Voir légendes en langue anglaise.

G1: Uniformes et équipements de combat standard, avec chevrons indiquant le grade au-dessus de la poche de poitrine gauche. Même camouflage sur la couverture de casque que sur la Planche H1. **G2:** La casquette et la toque tricotée étaient portées fréquemment. Poches supplémentaires portées sur la ceinture par des mitrailleurs. Paquetage d'assaut léger, à l'avant-plan, sanglé à des bretelles.

H1: Kepi rigide et veste ouatée avec insigne de grade sur la poitrine portée seulement par les officiers supérieurs. **H2:** Béret gris-bleu de l'Infanterie de Marine; parka ouaté, vêtement de protection standard des troupiers; les chevrons rouges sont censés être l'apanage des Marines. **H3, H4:** Présumés être des Commandos Marine d'après les photos en couleurs; notez le brevet de parachutiste au-dessus de l'insigne de grade d'officier sur la poitrine. Un gilet à poches a remplacé le harnais d'équipement individuel. Notez la baïonnette d'aspect archaïque portée par cette unité. **H5:** L'unité qui a joué le rôle de fer de lance pour l'invasion du 2 avril. Remarquez la mitraillette Sterling à silencieux, le blouson capitonné et le harnais individuel.

Farbtafeln

A1: Abgesehen vom neuen 'Fibre' Fallschirmjägerhelm könnte dieser Mann allen möglichen Abteilungen der Spezialeinheit engehören. Windundurchlässiger Parka und Überhose; persönliche Ausrüstung vom Typ 58, Wasserflasche vom Typ 44, neuer Nylon-Rucksack mit Schaufel und Poncho-Rolle, SLR-Gewehr mit Trilux-Visier. Mit zusätzlicher Munition und Waffen kann das Gesamtgewicht mehr als 50kg betragen. **A2:** Ranginsignien vorne auf der Mütze sind eine Eigenheit der Royal Marine; man beachte an erdem die Schlaufe für Ranginsignien aur der Vorderseite des windundurchlässigen Parkas (ebenfalls auf dem Rücken). **A3:** Die ursprüngliche Marine-Garnison trug im April noch Sommerkleidung—DPM-Kittel, grüne Hose, grünes RM-Barett, dunkles Abzeichen. Er hält eine 84mm Panzerabwehrwaffe, mit der er das argentinische Kriegsschiff 'Granville' beschädigte.

B2: Windundurchlässiger Parka mit Schlaufe für Rangabzeichen auf hellblauem Hintergrund (Regimentsfarbe). Regimentsbarett. **B2:** 'Fibre'-Helm mit Tarnhülle; Fallschirmjägerkittel, windundurchlässige Überhose; windundurchlässiger Parka über das Gepäck gehängt. Nur am rechten Arm: 'Brevet' der Fallschirmjäger, über dem blauen Abzeichen dieses Bataillons, über dem Rangwinkel. **B3:** Gewehr vom Typ Lee-Enfield .303 Nr. 4 für Heckenschützenfeuer umgestellt; Stahlhelm mit viel Tarnung; besonders grosser Kampfkittel mit zahlreichen Flicken, Sackleinen usw. aufgenäht.

C1: Drei GPMG in jedem Zug. Grüner regendichter Kittel mit weissem Futter, an einige Truppen ausgegeben. **C2:** Bren-Maschinengewehr auf 7,62mm Kaliber umgestellt, gelegentlich noch getragen. Die Marine hat windundurchlässige Parkas, olivgrüne Hose, wasserdichte Zivilgamaschen. **C3:** Khakifarbenes Barett der Foot Guards; 'CW'-Parka und Hose. Vorräte von Browning M2 0,50 cal. Gewehre mit kurzem Lauf wurde in aller Eile für zusätzliche Flugabwehr verteilt, sie wurde auch in den letzten Schlachten gegen feindliche Schützengräben eingesetzt.

D1: Von Flugabwehr-Einheiten der Royal Artillery benutzt; die Rakete erreicht Mach 2-Geschwindigkeit und eine Höhe bis zu 16.000 Fuss. **D2:** Von beiden Seiten in diesem Krieg benutzt, 'Blowpipe', ebenfalls wine Waffe der Royal Artillery, zum Feuern auf Flugzeuge, die frontal auf den Schützen zukommen, weniger für Verfolgungsjagden gedacht. **D3:** Die 'Artilleriewaffen des Infanteriebataillons', vom Minenwerfer-Zug der Hilfswaffenkompanie des Bataillons eingesetzt. Die Mannschaft trägt regendichten Anzug, 'CW'-Hose und Mütze, Barett der Welsh Guards. **D4:** Panzerabwehr-Rakete, von Infanteriebataillonen mit durchschlagendem Erfolg gegen feindliche Schützengräben eingesetzt.

E1: Scharlachrotes Barett der RMP; normaler Kampfkittel mit Fallschirmjäger-'Brevet' auf Armbinde (zeigt wahrscheinlich an, dassdieser Mann zu einer RMP-Abordnung mit Luftlandebataillon gehört), über dem Rangwinkel und das MP-Abzeichen. Viele Männer tragen wasserdichte 'Galoschen' über den Stiefeln. **E2:** Alle Gurkhas tragen dunkelgrünes Barett und andere Insignien in Farben des 'Rifle regiment'.

F1: Maj.Gen. Moore von den Royal Marines trug diese Mütze (Ursprung unbekannt) mit seinen Rang-Insignien auf der Vorderseite. **F2:** Marine-Einheiten haben Ärzte von der Royal Navy; Royal Navy-Abzeichen auf dem grünen Barett bedeutet, da der Träger den Kommando-Kurs absolviert hat; Rang-Insignien des Stabsarztes an der vorderen Schlaufe des windundurchlässigen Parkas. **F3:** Normaler DPM-Kampfkittel, windundurchlässige Überhose, 'Galoschen', gestrickter 'cap comforter' und gefütterte 'Nordirland'-Handschuhe. Schwarzes dreieckiges Schulterabzeichen gibt das Bataillon an, auf der anderen Schulter das Kompanieabzeichen: Kreis = C-Kompanie, Quadrat = B-Kompanie usw. Man beachte den Tarnüberzug über der Scheide des Kukri-Messers. **F4:** Barett des Parachute Regiment. **F5:** 'CW' ('Cold Weather') Mütze. Mützenabzeichen der eingesetzten Einheiten auf dem schmalen Hintergrund der Barettfarben—s. die englischen Bildunterschriften.

G1: Normaler Kampfanzug und-ausrüstung mit Rangwinkeln über der linken Brusttasche. Tarnung auf der Helmhülle wie in Tafel H1. **G2:** Mütze und gestrickte Toque waren weit verbreitet. MG-Schützen tragen zusätzliche Patronentaschen am Gürtel. Im Vordergrund leichtes Angriffsgepäck, hinter dem Schulter-Gurtwerk angeschnürt.

H1: Gestärkte Mütze und gesteppte Jacke mit Rang-Insignien auf der Brust (nur von Höheren Offizieren getragen). **H2:** Blau-graues Barett der Marine-Infanterie; gefütterter Parka, normale Schutzkleidung für Truppen; rote Winkel wahrscheinlich nur für Marines. **H3, H4:** Aufgrund des Farbfotos vermutlich als Marine-Kommando zu identifizieren; man beachte das Fallschirm-'Brevet' über den Rang-Insignien der Offiziere auf der Brust. Hemd mit Taschen anstelle von Gutwerk für persönliche Ausrüstung. Man beachte das archaisch aussehende Bajonett, das von dieser Einheit mit Sicherheit getragen wurde. **H5:** Die Einheit, die Invasion am 2. April anführte; man beachte die schallgedämpften Sterling-Maschinenpistole, gesteppte Weste und persönliches Gurtwerk (verschied von der herkömmlichen Ausführung).